I0410755

S. Hrg. 114–222

THE U.S.-AFRICA LEADERS SUMMIT SEVEN MONTHS LATER: PROGRESS AND SETBACKS

HEARING

BEFORE THE

SUBCOMMITTEE ON AFRICA AND GLOBAL HEALTH POLICY

OF THE

COMMITTEE ON FOREIGN RELATIONS UNITED STATES SENATE

ONE HUNDRED FOURTEENTH CONGRESS

FIRST SESSION

MARCH 19, 2015

Printed for the use of the Committee on Foreign Relations

Available via the World Wide Web: http://www.gpo.gov/fdsys/

U.S. GOVERNMENT PUBLISHING OFFICE

99–546 PDF   WASHINGTON : 2016

For sale by the Superintendent of Documents, U.S. Government Publishing Office
Internet: bookstore.gpo.gov   Phone: toll free (866) 512–1800; DC area (202) 512–1800
Fax: (202) 512–2104   Mail: Stop IDCC, Washington, DC 20402–0001

CONTENTS

(III)

THE U.S.–AFRICA LEADERS SUMMIT SEVEN MONTHS LATER: PROGRESS AND SETBACKS

THURSDAY, MARCH 19, 2015

U.S. SENATE,
SUBCOMMITTEE ON AFRICA AND GLOBAL HEALTH POLICY,
COMMITTEE ON FOREIGN RELATIONS,
Washington, DC.

The subcommittee met, pursuant to notice, at 9:37 a.m., in room SD–419, Dirksen Senate Office Building, Hon. Jeff Flake (chairman of the subcommittee) presiding.

Present: Senators Flake, Isakson, Markey, and Coons.

OPENING STATEMENT OF HON. JEFF FLAKE, U.S. SENATOR FROM ARIZONA

Senator FLAKE. This hearing of the Senate Foreign Relations Subcommittee on African Affairs and Global Health Policy will come to order.

I served as ranking member of this subcommittee for the past 2 years, but I have long had an interest in African affairs and have had the opportunity as we spoke to spend some time there, and it is an honor now to serve as chairman of this subcommittee, and to be able to examine some of the pressing needs on the continent that sometimes receive too little attention.

There seems to be a perpetual focus from the outside on foreign assistance to Africa, whether in helping to stop the spread of AIDS or Ebola, or providing humanitarian assistance to those suffering from drought, or to aid those who have been displaced due to a crisis. Much of this assistance is obviously critical. However, these countries want to develop their own economies and reach a point where they are not so dependent on foreign aid.

Africa is home to 6 of the 10 fastest-growing economies in the world. Real incomes across the continent have increased by 30 percent over the past 10 years. By 2040, Africa is expected to have a larger workforce than China.

In addition, sub-Saharan Africa's consumer base of nearly 1 billion people is rapidly growing and has the potential to create increased demand for U.S. goods, services, and technologies.

U.S. private-sector interest in tapping the economic potential of the continent is increasing, though our presence lags behind many of our partners and competitors in Europe and Asia.

Now, part of this discrepancy stems from a lack of opportunity in promising countries, and part stems from real challenges posed by weak governance and poor infrastructure in other countries.

Held last August, the U.S.-Africa Leaders Summit sought to highlight some of that promise and to address challenges to greater investment on the continent. The summit included the U.S.-Africa Business Forum, which brought together business leaders and heads of state, and provided a venue for U.S. investors to develop new business relationships on the continent. For companies with a long-standing presence in Africa, the day offered an opportunity to both reinforce relationships and discuss solutions to policy challenges.

Today's hearing will further explore the investment climate in Africa 7 months after the conclusion of the summit, and to look at policies that have emerged and policies that encourage or hinder the kind of growth that can lead to economic security on the continent.

We will hear from witnesses who are at the forefront of investing in Africa. We have invited them in order to hear firsthand about the potential for growth, as well as about the policies and practices, both on our part and on the part of Africans, that will create an attractive business climate.

In gathering ideas on how best to support market potential, we will hear from the Center for Global Development and the Council on Foreign Relations, two organizations that closely analyze economic growth in Africa.

Each of our witnesses today brings a unique perspective to the issue at hand, and I have no doubt they will contribute greatly to the debate. I thank you each for your time and for sharing your experience. I look forward to your testimony.

And with that, I will recognize the ranking member, Senator Markey, for his comments. I am glad to have Senator Markey on this committee. We served together in the House and traveled together, and we will work well together, I am sure, here.

STATEMENT OF HON. EDWARD J. MARKEY, U.S. SENATOR FROM MASSACHUSETTS

Senator MARKEY. And I know we will, Mr. Chairman. Thank you so much for recognizing me, and thank you so much for calling this very important hearing.

When Robert F. Kennedy met antiapartheid activists in South Africa in 1966, he famously said, "It is from numberless diverse acts of courage and belief that human history is shaped. Each time a man stands up for an ideal or acts to improve the lot of others or strikes out against injustice, he sends forth a tiny ripple of hope, and crossing each other from a million different centers of energy in daring, those ripples build a current that can sweep down the mightiest walls of oppression and resistance."

Inspired by those empowering words, I look forward to working with Senator Flake and the other members of this committee to add our own ripples of hope to the currents of change moving across Africa today.

In this subcommittee, I think we have several opportunities to have our actions ripple across countries an ocean away.

One, building a clean, affordable energy backbone in Africa. Power Africa is a critical part of improving the lives of millions of people in Africa and supporting economic development across the continent. Power Africa is starting strong as a Presidential initiative, and I am hopeful that this body can come up with a path forward to pass Energize Africa legislation and enshrine in U.S. law the importance of focusing on increasing access to electricity in Africa. I know Senator Coons has given great leadership on that issue, and I am looking forward to working with him and Senator Flake and other members of the committee.

Two, public health improvements. We need to focus on the improving health sector capacity across the continent so that the incredible gains of PEPFAR and other initiatives can continue, so that we can understand how to prevent the disastrous spread of diseases as basic as malaria and as crippling as Ebola.

Three, tiger poachers and their operations to protect wildlife. In recent years, poaching has taken a devastating toll on some of Africa's most iconic and imperiled wildlife. There is increasing evidence that some poaching is also helping to finance conflicts. It is critical that we do all that we can to prevent wildlife trafficking, including by finding those who finance it.

Four, work with African countries to provide for their own security and prevent the spread of nuclear bomb material. The summit highlighted new programs that seek to build Africa's peacekeeping response capacity, strengthen its institutions, focus on security, improve early warning systems for conflict. These are critical.

And finally, thanks to the work of the Center for Public Integrity and the Washington Post, we now have reason to be concerned about South Africa's stockpile of almost 500 pounds of highly enriched uranium, combined with concerns about Africa as a transit point for enriched uranium. South Africa's vulnerable stockpile is something that merits real attention.

Five, help prepare Africa for climate change. The Africa summit reiterated the Obama administration's support for increasing resilience among communities in all of the southern part of Africa that are already vulnerable to extreme weather. Climate change is not just super-charging blizzards in Boston. It is impacting floods in Malawi and forest fires in South Africa, and even worsening droughts like those in Somalia.

All of these issues must be discussed because they represent some of the central issues facing Africa today, where partnership with the American government and companies can drive progress.

Africa is a continent rich in economic and social potential. We must prioritize investment in Africa's future or our influence will wane in the wake of large commitments from Europe and China. And we must also ask how can we address the essential challenges that inhibit African nations' growth, because when people cannot access enough electricity to power homes, how can we expect their full participation in the local economy? When families cannot keep their children healthy because a constant battle with disease is occurring, how can parents put them in school or go to work? When natural disasters prevent the building of resilient communities, how can countries build resilient economies?

Today I hope to learn from our witnesses how the policy initiatives under the summit are proceeding. I think it is essential to know how this body can be helpful in paving the way for increased U.S. investment in Africa in a variety of arenas.

I thank you, Mr. Chairman, for calling this very important hearing.

Senator FLAKE. Thank you, Senator Markey.

I just wanted to note also how nice it is to have Senator Isakson here. He has long had an interest in Africa on a number of fronts and has traveled extensively on the continent, and I look forward to trying to tap his expertise as we go along here.

We will be joined, I am sure, by Senator Coons and some others as we go along.

Let us turn now to the witnesses.

Our first witness is Mr. Ben Leo. Mr. Leo is a senior fellow at the Center for Global Development and the director of the Rethinking U.S. Development Policy initiative. This initiative seeks to broaden the U.S. Government's approach to development, including the full range of investment, trade, and technology policies, while also strengthening existing foreign assistance tools. Mr. Leo's research primarily focuses on the rapidly changing development finance environment, with particular emphasis on private capital flows, infrastructure, and debt dynamics. In addition, he is testing a range of new technological methods for collecting high-frequency information about citizens' development priorities.

Our second witness will be Del Renigar. Mr. Renigar is GE Corporate's senior counsel for Global Government Affairs and Policy. He advises all GE businesses on public policy, trade, investment, national security, and government relations issues in Africa, the Middle East and South Asia. Mr. Renigar also serves as the staff representative to the President's Advisory Committee on Doing Business in Africa. Before joining GE, Del served as the Director of International Economics for the Western Hemisphere on the National Security Council, and as the Senior Counsel to the General Counsel and Deputy Secretary of the U.S. Department of Commerce, where he counseled the Office of the Secretary, the Bureau of Industry and Security, and the International Trade Administration on trade, foreign policy, and national security issues.

Our third witness will be Susan Tuttle. Ms. Tuttle is currently the director of Middle East and Africa for IBM's Government and Regulatory Affairs Office, and has geographic responsibility for initiatives to support IBM's business and expansion efforts across Africa and the Middle East. Over her 30-year career with IBM, Ms. Tuttle has worked with governments all over the world on public policy issues related to technology and innovation, with key focus on skills and talent development, research, IPR, market access and trade and policy-related infrastructure. Ms. Tuttle is on the Board of Directors and the Executive Committee of the Corporate Council on Africa and chairs its ICT Working Group. She is also on the Board of Directors for GlobalWIN, the Global Women's Innovation Network.

Our fourth witness is Tom Bollyky. Mr. Bollyky is senior fellow for Global Health, Economics, and Development at the Council on Foreign Relations. He is also an adjunct professor of law at Georgetown University and a consultant to the Bill and Melinda Gates Foundation. Prior to joining CFR, Mr. Bollyky was a fellow at the Center for Global Development, and Director of Intellectual Property and Pharmaceutical Policy at the Office of the U.S. Trade Representative. He was also a Fulbright Scholar to South Africa, where he worked as a staff attorney at the AIDS Law Project on treatment access issues related to HIV/AIDS.

Thank you all for being here. I think we all recognize what expertise you all carry, and it is significant.

We remind you that your full statements will be included in the record. If you could keep your comments to close to 5 minutes, that would be great so we can allow time for questioning from all of our members.

With that, Mr. Leo.

STATEMENT OF BEN LEO, SENIOR FELLOW, DIRECTOR OF RETHINKING U.S. DEVELOPMENT POLICY, CENTER FOR GLOBAL DEVELOPMENT, WASHINGTON, DC

Mr. LEO. Thank you, Chairman Flake, Ranking Member Markey, and Senator Isakson.

This hearing is very well timed following the Leaders summit last year and several issues that Congress will be considering this year such as AGOA reauthorization and the Energize and Electrify Africa Acts.

My remarks focus on three major U.S. policy gaps and how Congress can help to address them. These include passing Energize and Electrify Africa legislation; two, modernizing U.S. development finance tools; and three, urging the administration to negotiate more investment treaties.

Each of these pose no incremental budgetary cost and reflect a simple fact: private investment is key to African growth and U.S. policy objectives in this increasingly important region.

African growth has averaged about 5 percent a year since 2000, exceeding levels in many other regions. FDI has increased sixfold, and inflation, which is historically a major problem, is dramatically lower than it was in the 1980s and 1990s. The region has a promising future despite many challenges, and will be home to new emerging major markets such as Nigeria, Ethiopia, and Kenya.

Above all else, Africans increasingly desire an American partner that helps to deliver economic opportunities primarily through greater trade and investment.

U.S. Government approaches such as Power Africa are starting to reflect these realities, but much more is needed. Most U.S. aid programs are simply not designed or equipped to address these shifting realities. We need to emphasize new tools that promote U.S. investment and leverage America's greatest strengths.

Emerging actors such as China understand these dynamics extremely well. The question is whether we are ready and willing to compete.

First, Congress should pass Energize and Electrify Africa legislation. Such action would send a very strong signal to African leaders, businesses and people that the United States is a strategic and long-term partner. Unreliable and costly electricity is a major competitiveness and human development constraint in nearly every African country. President Obama's Power Africa initiative is doing very important work to address this. Yet, there is a risk of losing momentum, particularly after the current administration leaves office.

Passing authorizing legislation would make it a durable bipartisan effort. This legislation should include clear reporting targets, multiyear authorization for OPIC, and an exemption from carbon cap rules for the poorest, lowest emitting countries.

Second, Congress should modernize U.S. development finance tools by creating a U.S. Development Finance Corporation, or a USDFC. America's finance development institution, OPIC, is a little-known development agency that provides seed capital and risk insurance for U.S. investors entering emerging markets. It operates on a self-sustaining basis, and it has provided net transfers to the U.S. Treasury for nearly 40 consecutive years. Yet, it is underutilized, has not really adapted since the 1970s, and is hamstrung by outdated or misdirected restrictions.

Beyond OPIC, many other U.S. investment tools are spread across numerous agencies, which leads to bureaucratic fights, inefficiencies and delays.

A reformed and enhanced OPIC would form the foundation of the USDFC, and it would bring together all the capabilities that are scattered across the U.S. Government. Importantly, this is about consolidating existing tools, making them better, and delivering better results. It is all at no incremental cost to U.S. taxpayers.

It is not about bigger government or corporate welfare. It is about making what we have better. This proposal would require bold congressional leadership. Yet, by simultaneously reforming OPIC and providing it with consolidated authorities, the U.S. Government would ensure that its development finance tools are fit for today's global needs.

Third, Congress should urge the Obama administration to pursue legally binding bilateral investment treaties, or BITs. These treaties encourage investment by providing investors with protections against things like expropriation or fickle legal systems. However, the United States has only ratified six agreements to date with African countries, covering a mere 7 percent of regional GDP.

Countries like China and Canada have demonstrated that African governments are ready and willing to sign these agreements. While Beijing and Ottawa have been busy inking new deals, USTR has been pursuing ineffectual, non-legally-binding trade and investment framework agreements. It is time to stop allocating scarce resources to these talk shops and start negotiating real agreements that have impact for U.S. investors and on promoting economic growth in the region.

In conclusion, private investment is key to African growth and ensuring that the region's growing youth bulge finds meaningful opportunities. It matters for our security, it matters for our commercial policy and our foreign policy. If we fail to act on this agenda and build real momentum after the Leaders summit, then America's influence and relevance will be further eroded. There is no question that other actors such as China will fill America's leadership void.

Thank you very much.

[The prepared statement of Mr. Leo follows:]

PREPARED STATEMENT OF BEN LEO

Thank you, Chairman Flake, Ranking Member Markey, and other members of the subcommittee. I appreciate the opportunity to appear before you today to discuss the potential for greater U.S. trade and investment with sub-Saharan Africa. This hearing sends an important message about Congress' focus on expanding private sector-based development approaches in this increasingly strategic region. It is particularly well timed following the historic U.S.-Africa Leaders Summit last August and several issues that the 114th Congress will be considering this year, including the African Growth and Opportunity Act and the Energize/Electrify Africa Act.

Within this broader context, my testimony will briefly highlight some of the most obvious gaps in our current approach, along with key opportunities and challenges. I also outline three specific policy recommendations for your consideration, including:

(1) Congress should urge the administration to pursue legally binding Bilateral Investment Treaties (BITs). Such action will promote greater U.S. investment flows to the continent while also positioning U.S. investors on equal footing with European, Chinese, and other investors who benefit from BIT protections.

(2) Congress should modernize U.S. development finance tools by creating a modern U.S. Development Finance Corporation (USDFC). This budget-neutral reform would ensure that U.S. policy tools better respond to developing countries' priorities and emphasize private sector-based development models. More modest reforms to the Overseas Private Investment Corporation would be beneficial even if Congress does not move forward with a USDFC.

(3) Congress should pass Energize/Electrify Africa legislation that promotes U.S. investment in the power sector and improves economic opportunities along with health and education outcomes. Such action would send a strong signal to African leaders, businesses, and people that the United States is a strategic and long-term partner.

THE NEW U.S.–AFRICA NARRATIVE—RHETORIC AND POLICY REALITY

Last August, the U.S. Government turned an important page in its relationship with sub-Saharan Africa. President Obama and his administration declared that they were listening to the priorities of African governments, businesses, and people. The official U.S.-Africa Leaders Summit agenda naturally covered a broad spectrum of issues. However, the central narrative was delivered with succinct clarity. America finally has awoken to the growing economic opportunity and importance of sub-Saharan Africa. While the main summit takeaways were largely rhetorical, this shift in mindset should not be underestimated.

Overall, Africa projects a promising future despite global and localized headwinds. Regional GDP growth has averaged 5 percent annually since 2000, exceeding levels in Latin America, Central Asia, and the Middle East. Foreign direct investment has increased nearly sixfold, and is now rapidly expanding into consumer and service sectors. Macroeconomic management, such as controlling inflation, has vastly improved compared to the 1980s and the 1990s. Even with falling commodity prices, growth is projected to remain strong over the near- and medium-term.

Above all else, most Africans desire an American partner that is focused on helping to deliver economic opportunities, primarily through greater trade and private investment flows. Roughly 70 percent of surveyed Africans cite economic issues—such as jobs and infrastructure—as their most pressing priorities.[1] These priorities transcend geographic, gender, and age divides. These views, expressed by ordinary Africans given a voice through representative surveys, contrast sharply with how most Americans view the continent. After decades of depressing media coverage, we might expect Africans to overwhelmingly prioritize humanitarian needs, such as basic health care, education, and food security. That is not the picture emerging from much of Africa. The U.S.-Africa Leaders Summit made it clear that the U.S. Government has begun to internalize these shifting dynamics.

Figure 1 – Jobs, Income, and Infrastructure Dominate African Concerns

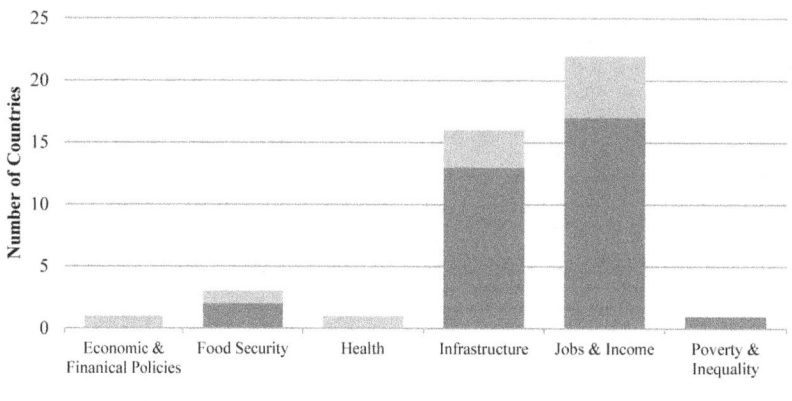

Source: Afrobarometer

Despite immense opportunities, many African economies remain constrained by poor business climates, small market size, and collusive political economy dynamics. Among the greatest barriers to growth are unreliable and costly electricity; high transport costs; inadequate access to finance; and burdensome regulations and corruption. The responsibility for confronting these challenges rests squarely with African governments, and their citizens who must hold them accountable. Yet, the U.S. Government can play a strategic supporting role in helping to address them.

While the Leaders summit suggests that U.S. officials have started to internalize the Africa Rising reality, even amidst regional threats and challenges, actual Obama administration policy and ongoing messaging has been much slower to adapt. Judged solely by White House and State Department press statements and social media feeds, casual observers might believe that America's top continent-wide priorities are combatting wildlife trafficking and LGBT discrimination. The question is not whether these kinds of issues should be raised and discussed with America's partners in the region. Instead, the question is whether they should dominate the post-summit rhetoric emanating from Washington and its senior government officials, when these issues do not appear anywhere near the top of African nations' priorities, whether Americans like it or not. Particularly in light of the proposed new framework for U.S.-Africa relations, which revolves around a private sector-based partnership that is supported and enabled by respective governments.

Going forward, Congress should push the Obama administration to deepen and accelerate its emerging U.S.-Africa narrative through several strategic steps. This includes: (1) pressuring the administration to launch an ambitious round of BIT negotiations with African nations; (2) overhauling U.S. development finance tools; and (3) passing landmark legislation focused on African energy poverty issues. Africa has always been a region that attracts broad bipartisan support. There is both an opportunity, and an urgent need, to advance this agenda. If we fail to act and continue to build real momentum after the Leaders summit, then America's influence and relevance will be eroded in an increasingly multipolar world. There is no question that other actors, such as China and other emerging nations, will fill America's leadership void, and capitalize on their closer alignment with the continent's agenda.

RECOMMENDATION 1: UTILIZE BILATERAL INVESTMENT TREATIES
AS A LOW–COST POLICY TOOL

Bilateral investment treaties have long been low-cost policy tools for promoting investment, both among developed and developing countries. From a development and commercial policy perspective, BITs can encourage investment by providing foreign investors with core protections against political risk and uncertain business environments, such as expropriation, discriminatory treatment, or weak and partial legal systems. According to UNCTAD, there are now over 3,200 investment agreements globally, including almost 300 involving African nations. In addition, many

African governments are negotiating BITs with their neighbors, such as Mauritius, which has signed or ratified agreements with 17 African countries since 2000.

Many econometric studies find that BITs have a positive and significant impact on promoting foreign direct investment (FDI) flows to developing countries.[2] While BITs clearly are not a silver bullet, the potential return on U.S. Government action is very high. This is due to their low-cost nature, which only includes salaries and travel budgets for U.S. Government negotiators. BITs pose no costs to U.S. taxpayers beyond these modest expenses.

Despite these benefits, the United States is lagging far behind European, Asian, and other emerging market players when it comes to negotiating BITs with African countries. Currently, the United States has only six agreements in place, which include: Cameroon (1989), the Democratic Republic of Congo (1989), Republic of Congo (1994), Mozambique (2005), Rwanda (2012), and Senegal (1990). Collectively, these treaties cover a mere 7 percent of regional GDP. Even if the United States completed hoped for agreements with Mauritius and the East African Community, which have been under consideration for several years, regional coverage rates would remain extremely low at roughly 15 percent. To date, the Obama administration has not signed a single investment agreement anywhere in the world.

Other capital-exporting countries, such as China and Canada, demonstrate that African governments are ready and willing to sign investment promotion agreements. China has signed investment treaties with 24 African countries, including 15 out of the largest 20 regional economies. Once all of these agreements are ratified, China will have legally binding agreements covering almost 80 percent of regional GDP. In addition, Canada has signed BITs with eight African countries in the last few years. This includes the region's economic powerhouse, Nigeria, whose roughly $600 billion economy is larger than Malaysia and Vietnam combined.[3] In addition, Canada has several more negotiations underway, such as with Ghana and Kenya. Canada's rapid progress has been driven by Prime Minister Harper's strong commitment to advance BITs as a core commercial and development policy tool. If the Obama administration demonstrated a similar level of political support and ambition, whether on its own or pushed by Congress, the United States could achieve similar progress.

**Figure 2 – US BIT Coverage Lags Far Behind Other Investing Nations --
% of Sub-Saharan Africa's GDP Covered by Investment Treaties**

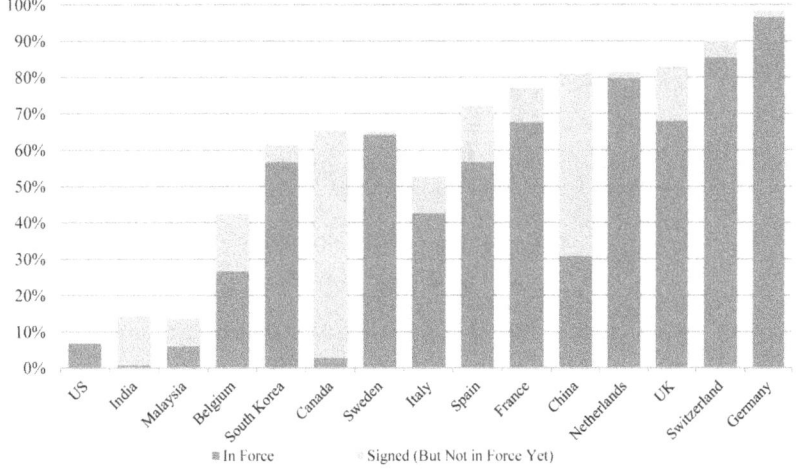

Source: UNCTAD, IMF World Economic Outlook database

The U.S. Government should address the new Model BIT's complexity, which could limit our ability to conclude negotiations with many African countries. In 2012, the United States unveiled a new template agreement, which sought to address past concerns raised by labor unions, environmental groups, other NGOs, as well as some developing countries that wish to retain more public policy sovereignty and flexibility. As a result, the 42-page template now affords more government discretion than in the past, which is one reason it is so complex. For example, it exempts government actions (except "in rare circumstances") to protect health, labor, and consumer safety from investors' protections against expropriation. These modifications have broadened U.S. political support for this policy tool. Yet, the U.S. Government will need to consider ways of addressing the practical challenges posed by an increasingly complex template agreement. There are two concrete options for doing so. First, USAID could provide targeted bilateral technical assistance for countries engaging in BIT negotiations, as it did with the U.S.-Central American Free Trade Agreement (U.S.–CAFTA). Second, the U.S. Government could provide modest financial contributions to multilateral facilities, such as the Africa Legal Support Facility, which is housed at the African Development Bank.

Going forward, Congress should pressure the administration to stop investing in ineffectual Trade and Investment Framework Agreements (TIFAs) and start investing in BIT negotiations. Over the last decade, USTR has focused almost solely on pursuing TIFAs in sub-Saharan Africa, which provide no binding protections for U.S. investors and do not advance a real reform agenda. This misplaced and non-strategic effort has distracted limited U.S. Government attention from pursuing real negotiations with African nations. Put differently, while China, Canada, and other nations have been signing countless legally binding treaties, the United States has been signing TIFAs that provide no tangible benefit to U.S. investors and companies. It is time to stop allocating scarce resources to these inconsequential talk shops and move toward pursuing real agreements that catalyze much needed (and wanted) investment flows.

Figure 3 – The Obama Administration Has Failed to Sign Any Investment Agreements Despite Historical Bipartisan Progress

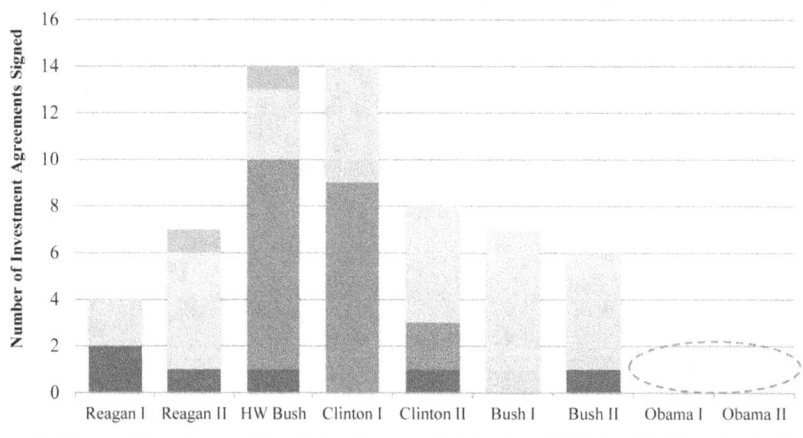

RECOMMENDATION 2: REFORM AND UNLEASH U.S. DEVELOPMENT FINANCE TOOLS

There is an urgent need to implement targeted reforms that would improve the effectiveness, impact, and scale of U.S. development finance institutions. In many ways, the future of development policy lies in development finance. This reflects a number of new dynamics, including: growing citizen and business demand, entry of new emerging market actors, a shift toward private sector-oriented development models, and the declining importance of foreign aid. As noted previously, foreign government partners are increasingly focused on attracting private investment, especially in infrastructure and productive sectors. Nearly every national development strategy includes a strong emphasis on attracting investment for physical infrastructure (e.g., electricity and transport) and labor-intensive sectors such as agriculture and services. Currently, most U.S. aid programs are not designed, structured, or equipped to address these shifting needs.

The primary U.S. development finance institution, the Overseas Private Investment Corporation (OPIC), is a highly constrained and underutilized tool. OPIC's mission is to promote U.S. development, commercial, and foreign policy objectives through private investment abroad. It is a remarkably effective tool for U.S. policy given its constraints. It provides U.S. investors in developing countries with debt financing, loan guarantees, political risk insurance, and support for private-equity investment funds when private actors cannot. It operates on a self-sustaining basis and has provided positive net transfers to the U.S. Treasury for nearly 40 consecutive years. Since its inception, OPIC has helped mobilize more than $200 billion of U.S. investment through more than 4,000 development-related projects. However, a modernized, scaled-up OPIC is desperately needed as U.S. development policy moves beyond aid.

With few exceptions, OPIC has not evolved since its establishment in 1971. This means that OPIC has been unable to adapt its model to changing market-based demands and/or adequately address some of its past critiques (see details below). For instance, OPIC remains highly constrained by inadequate staffing and outdated authorities. It must rely on congressional appropriations to cover annual administrative expenses (e.g., salaries, travel, and office space), despite generating operating profits on a consistent basis. This de facto constraint has prevented OPIC from fully leveraging its existing capital base in support of U.S. development and foreign policy objectives. In practical terms, this means that roughly $11 billion in development capital remains locked away while more and more U.S. investors are seeking assistance to enter frontier markets, such as Nigeria, Ghana, and Kenya.[4]

Other traditional players have adapted their development finance tools and are leaving the United States far behind. Well-established European development finance institutions (DFIs) are providing integrated services for businesses, which cover debt and equity financing, risk mitigation, and technical assistance. These European institutions, such as the Netherlands FMO or Germany's DEG, were not originally designed this way. Instead, they have been reformed over the course of decades to ensure that their tools match the needs of investors, businesses, and overall development objectives. The U.S. Government, including Congress, can learn from these experiences and push through a number of targeted reforms.

Many emerging market nations have accelerated the trend by establishing development finance vehicles. It is not just European institutions that are pushing ahead. Many emerging market actors—including China, India, Brazil, and Malaysia—have dramatically increased financing activities in developing regions, such as sub-Saharan Africa, Latin America, and East Asia. The $50 billion Asian Infrastructure Investment Bank, championed by China, has been in the headlines recently. However, it is far from the only example. The $50 billion BRICs Bank, also driven by China, is expected to provide additional alternatives for African nations.

The time has come for a U.S. Development Finance Corporation (USDFC) that would harness America's three greatest strengths: innovation and technology, entrepreneurship, and a deep capital base. My colleague Todd Moss and I have outlined this idea in significant detail in a new Center for Global Development paper released this week.[5] Other think tanks (e.g., Brookings Institute, CSIS, and Council on Foreign Relations), the President's Global Development Council, and private foundations and academics have all advocated similar proposals.[6] This is a big idea whose time is now.

A reformed and enhanced OPIC would form the foundation of this strategic institution. It also would consolidate a number of other investment-related tools that are scattered across USAID, the U.S. Trade and Development Agency, and other U.S. development agencies. Importantly, the new USDFC would be financially self-sustaining and managed according to market-based metrics.

The USDFC will require bold congressional leadership and a number of targeted reforms. These reforms also would address historical critiques of OPIC, such as the appearance of providing corporate welfare and/or crowding out private capital. By simultaneously reforming this pivotal institution and providing it with new authorities and flexibility, the U.S. Government would ensure that its development finance tools are fit for purpose in the 21st century.

- *Explicit project approval criteria to ensure that private capital is crowded in, not displaced or crowded out.* Specifically, the USDFC Board of Directors should receive and consider documentation illustrating that the proposed project would not proceed without USDFC support. Such action is essential for avoiding any appearance of corporate welfare. In turn, the institution should report annually on the so-called "additionality" of its operations. In practical terms, this means documenting how its project-level activities helped to catalyze and unlock private sources of capital that would not have happened without USDFC involvement.

- *A presumption of public disclosure on its operational activities and development impact.* There should be a high bar for withholding information due to commercial confidentiality concerns. At a minimum, the institution should publish all project description summaries and project-level development performance data on an annual basis. Such actions would enhance public accountability.

- *Flexible portfolio and staffing levels that uphold rigorous performance and financial management standards.* The institution should not have an ex-ante portfolio target size. Instead, it should have sufficient flexibility to support investments that demonstrate strong development impact, prudently managed financial risks, and clear "additionality" vis-a-vis private sector alternatives. To ensure rigorous congressional oversight, performance metrics covering each of these areas should be reported regularly to the appropriate committees.

The aforementioned reforms should be actively considered for OPIC even if Congress does not establish a consolidated U.S. Development Finance Corporation. Each of these changes would improve OPIC's operational effectiveness, address past critiques, and enhance public accountability. Therefore, they should be pursued even if Congress does not consolidate other agencies' investment-related tools or provide additional authorities.

RECOMMENDATION 3: PASS THE ENERGIZE AFRICA/ELECTRIFY AFRICA LEGISLATION TO HELP ADDRESS BINDING ENERGY ACCESS CONSTRAINTS ACROSS THE CONTINENT

Unreliable and costly electricity is a major competitiveness and human development constraint in nearly every African country. Roughly 600 million Africans lack access to any form of modern electricity, which greatly reduces economic opportunities as well as health and education outcomes. Half of African firms cite electricity as a major constraint on their competitiveness, profitability, and expansion potential. In some African economies, losses from power outages amount to more than 10 percent of sales. In addition, greater than 80 percent of firms in Ghana, Tanzania, and Uganda cite concerns with power reliability and affordability.

Figure 4 – African Firms Citing Electricity as Major Constraint, Select Countries

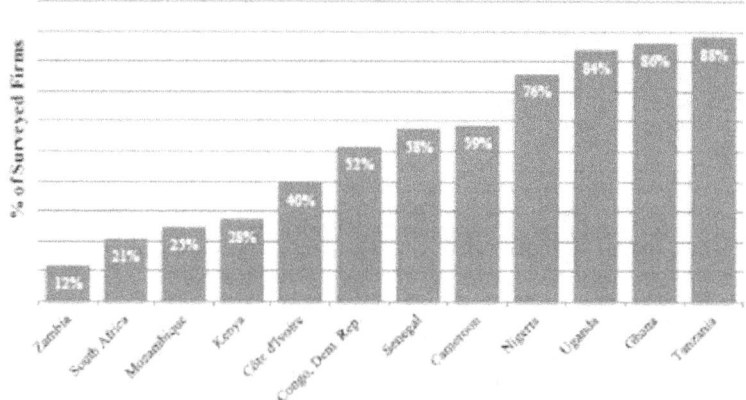

Source: World Bank Business Enterprise surveys

The further expansion of the Power Africa Initiative was the most tangible outcome from the U.S.-Africa Leaders Summit. Based on early progress, President Obama announced a tripling of the original Power Africa targets. The initiative now aims to deliver 30,000 megawatts of power generation capacity and new connections for at least 60 million households and businesses. Unofficially, this could mean up to 300 million people acquiring access to reliable and affordable electricity over time (average household size = ~5 people). These are bold targets and President Obama should be commended for setting them.

U.S. development agencies—including USAID, OPIC, and the MCC—have made tangible progress in implementing the Power Africa vision. Public sector commitments total over $7 billion, mostly from OPIC and the U.S. Export-Import Bank, plus some USAID technical assistance. This has helped to catalyze over $20 billion in private capital from power development companies and investors. The initiative also has leveraged additional investment from other official actors, including $5 billion from the World Bank and $1 billion from Sweden.

The Power Africa team has been strategic in where and how it has deployed scarce U.S. taxpayer resources. USAID has used grant resources selectively, targeting them on sector-level reforms that would enable massive private investments.

Supporting Nigeria's power sector privatization plans is a noteworthy illustration. Moreover, USAID, the Commerce Department, and OPIC partnered with leading power developers and legal scholars to develop a model power purchase agreement that could dramatically reduce the amount of time required to bring generation projects to closure. These activities do not garner much public attention, but they have the potential to deliver massive practical impact with very little U.S. taxpayer money.

In addition, the Obama administration is rightly focusing on measuring its impact across a range of areas. All effective Presidential initiatives—such as PEPFAR, the President's Malaria Initiative, and the MCC—have one thing in common. They have an overriding focus on measuring, tracking, and evaluating the impact of their activities. Power Africa has an initial plan in place, and its core team is thoughtfully developing a comprehensive and rigorous long-term monitoring and evaluation plan. This is not a straightforward exercise given data deficiencies in much of the region. Nonetheless, I am hopeful that they will come forward with a practical plan of action soon that will help to keep the relevant U.S. Government agencies accountable going forward.

Further Power Africa progress will partly depend on finding permanent solutions to well-intended, but ineffectual and harmful, U.S. investment regulations. The lack of multiyear congressional authorization for OPIC has put the agency (and U.S. investors), tasked with negotiating complex long-term infrastructure deals, in a state of uncertainty. OPIC has also been unable to reliably support a diversified mix of power generation projects. A carbon emissions cap has effectively pushed the agency out of all natural gas projects in the world's poorest countries. Meanwhile, many African countries are actively exploring for and developing natural gas deposits, which would deliver low-cost and reliable fuel sources. The cap (temporarily lifted in the FY14 and FY15 Appropriations Acts) is undermining Power Africa's potential and dampening U.S. investment abroad. Meanwhile, it is making no meaningful impact on carbon mitigation objectives. All of sub-Saharan Africa accounts for roughly 2 percent of current global carbon emissions. Even if all African countries adopted zero carbon strategies, it would have almost no impact on global targets. And in the meantime, millions of people in poor countries would be denied access to life-transforming electricity. There are practical compromise options to address this divisive issue.[6]

Going forward, Congress should strengthen and formalize Power Africa through authorizing legislation, which includes clear reporting targets, multiyear authorization for OPIC, and an exemption from carbon cap rules for the poorest, low-emitting countries. The greatest risk right now is that U.S. momentum will recede after the current administration leaves office. Energy poverty is too long term and too critical an issue to allow that to happen. Passing authorization legislation would make it a durable U.S. development effort and ensure that energy poverty remains at the top of the U.S.-Africa agenda.

CONCLUSION

The U.S.-Africa Leaders Summit was an important moment for our relationship with this increasingly important region. While the summit had a clear emphasis on promoting economic engagement, largely through greater trade and investment, the subsequent impact on actual U.S. Government policy and messaging has been mixed. The Power Africa initiative is a noteworthy example of where ongoing U.S. activities are meaningful and strongly aligned with Africans' priorities.

Congress should advance U.S. efforts to promote economic engagement and development priorities in the region, and push the Obama administration to do more. First, it should urge the administration to negotiate legally binding Bilateral Investment Treaties (BITs) with African nations. Second, Congress should consider creating a U.S. Development Finance Corporation or pursuing more modest reforms that would improve and unleash the Overseas Private Investment Corporation (OPIC). Third, Congress should pass Energize/Electrify Africa legislation that promotes U.S. investment in the power sector and seeks to improve economic opportunities along with health and education outcomes. None of these actions entail additional budgetary outlays. Instead, they are strategic, results-based policy tools that would give a significant boost to U.S.-Africa relations.

End Notes

[1] Benjamin Leo, Robert Morello, and Vijaya Ramachandran (2015). "The Face of African Infrastructure: Service Availability and Citizens' Demands," Working Paper 393, Center for Global Development, Washington DC.

[2] For instance, Egger and Pfaffermayr (2004), Peinhardt and Allee (2007), and Haftel (2010) find that BITs consistently increase FDI between the associated countries once they are signed and ratified. Salacuse and Sullivan (2005) find that the presence of a U.S. BIT translates into increased FDI to a given country in a given year by 77 percent to 85 percent. Savant and Sachs (2009) argue that foreign investors with exposure to extractive industries often rely on BITs because of the historical experience of host governments behaving in a discriminatory or even predatory fashion. Busse, Königer, and Nunnenkamp (2010) find that BITs likely substitute for weak domestic institutions in developing countries. However, there are other studies that do not find that BITs have a statistically significant impact on FDI flows. These differing empirical results appear to be driven largely by methodological challenges. First, BITs can vary substantially in terms of the quality of investor protections and industry sector coverage. An investment treaty with watered down provisions or large sector carve-outs arguably would have a smaller impact on promoting FDI flows. Second, in some instances, it is difficult to clearly establish whether specific BITs were focused on promoting new foreign investment or on protecting existing FDI stocks after the fact.

[3] Malaysia and Vietnam are two prospective signatories to the Trans-Pacific Partnership (TPP) agreement, with which the U.S. currently does not have either a BIT or FTA investment chapter in place. Brunei, Japan, and New Zealand are the only other TPP countries without a U.S. investment agreement.

[4] Under existing congressionally approved authorities, OPIC has a maximum contingent liability limit of $29 billion. As of 2014, OPIC had committed roughly $18 billion of this maximum limit. This means that OPIC could provide an additional $11 billion to support private investment transactions in developing countries.

[5] Ben Leo and Todd Moss (2015). "Bringing U.S. Development Finance into the 21st Century: Proposal for a Self-Sustaining, Full-Service US Development Finance Corporation," Center for Global Development.

[6] For additional details, see: (1) U.S. Global Development Council (2014), Beyond Business As Usual; (2) Brookings Institute (2013), "Strengthening U.S. Development Finance Institutions"; and (3) U.S. National Advisory Board on Impact Investing (2014), Private Capital, Public Good.

[7] For additional details, see Todd Moss, Roger Pielke, Jr., and Morgan Bazilian, "Balancing Energy Access and Environmental Goals in Development Finance: The Case of the OPIC Carbon Cap," CGD Policy Paper 38.

Senator FLAKE. Thank you, Mr. Leo.

Mr. Renigar.

STATEMENT OF DEL RENIGAR, SENIOR COUNSEL, GLOBAL GOVERNMENT AFFAIRS AND POLICY MIDDLE EAST, AFRICA AND INDIA, GE CORPORATION, WASHINGTON, DC

Mr. RENIGAR. Good morning. Thank you, Mr. Chairman. Thank you, Ranking Member Markey and Senator Isakson. It is a pleasure to be here.

My name is Del Renigar with General Electric. As you may know, GE has a rich history in Africa going back more than 100 years. Today, we have over 2,300 employees across 25 countries, and Africa has been one of our fastest growing regions in recent years for the entire company.

Given this history and these opportunities, GE sought to maximize its participation in the U.S.-Africa Leaders Summit, with more than 30 leaders in town from GE during that 1-week period. We hosted six major events, including an energy thought leadership conference with The Economist called "Africa Ascending." We announced more than $2 billion in investments in facility development, skills training, and new sustainability initiatives, and we held over 100 meetings with heads of state and ministers.

Key deliverables for GE related to the summit include several billion dollars in rail, power generation, health care, and aviation deals across the continent, as well as related scholarships, training, and technical support for African students, patients, workers, and health care professionals.

One I might highlight in particular is our work with mobile ultrasound, so-called V-Scans. We are working with midwives in Ghana and Nigeria to give them the training that they need so they can use this new mobile technology to provide health care in rural regions.

GE's engagement with the summit is ongoing. Our CEO for Africa, Jay Ireland, has been appointed to the President's Advisory Council on Doing Business in Africa, and we are actively working with the Commerce Department now in preparing recommendations on infrastructure.

Despite all of these good news stories, as you know, the continent suffers from extreme energy poverty that severely limits its growth and its development. But many African companies are taking steps to improve energy access. Afrisol Energy, a 4-year-old Kenyan company, is looking to turn waste into fuel to power Nairobi's slums and rural neighborhoods. This is but one of several African companies who have won awards and grants from GE, USAID, and the U.S.-Africa Development Foundation for innovations using renewable, distributed power solutions.

These and other distributed power solutions can help address the needs of Africa. These include small-scale power sources from 100 kilowatts to 100 megawatts that run on fuel from solar, from fuel cells, from gas, from diesel, and even wind.

To be clear, though, these distributed power solutions, even though they are quite strong in Africa, will only play a complementary role. Africa will still need centralized and large-scale gas and power grids in order to deal with urbanization and industrialization.

Building on these models, gas-to-power initiatives are a way to make power available to people who need it, especially in a place like Africa, which is endowed with 400 trillion cubic feet of gas reserves. We see a tremendous opportunity to use gas-to-power initiatives to address the energy access in Africa. The basic concept entails convening stakeholders, governments, developers, fuel suppliers, equipment providers and financiers to craft a workable, holistic approach to identifying and delivering gas resources to add new power generation capacity where it is needed.

The best example of this is in Ghana, the Ghana 1000 project. This is a signature Power Africa project that has involved an entire whole-of-government approach with MCC, USAID, Ex-Im, OPIC, and the U.S. Government as a whole. This project consists of a floating storage and regasification unit, the first in sub-Saharan Africa, and related infrastructure for the import and domestic use of LNG. This will be used to power over 1,300 megawatts of combined-cycle power in Western Ghana. This will have a long-term impact in Ghana and throughout the region because it will provide lower emissions, it will provide the first opportunity to use LNG in this way, it will displace diesel, and will also provide opportunities for distributed power, as well as powering regions and cities. When it is complete, we believe that the Ghana 1000 will be a model project that can be replicated across the continent.

Another place where we need to be focusing on gas-to-power is Nigeria. As you know, this is one of the largest countries on the continent, and they have some of the largest gas reserves in the world. Yet, they have very, very little power. There are a number of problems in their gas infrastructure. There is flaring. There is reinjection of gas going on as well.

The government has tried to implement a number of privatization initiatives to turn brown-field power plants into new projects and expand the power there, but they are running into a number of obstacles. Investors are beginning to get concerned. This is an area that we have to pay particular attention to if we are going to address energy access in Africa.

The opportunities here for the U.S. Government are significant. What we see is really a need for government to see projects through from beginning to end. It is not so much the physical barriers but the procedural barriers that are hanging up projects in sub-Saharan Africa.

One particular issue that we need to talk about is the issue of finance. These projects do need finance, and that means Ex-Im and OPIC. These are programs that we have used around Africa. Our customers value these, the African governments value these programs, and we believe that with more flexibility and more reform, that OPIC and Ex-Im can continue to play an important role in developing these projects. We urge the Congress, we urge the administration to renew these important programs.

There are a number of other initiatives going on that support this. MCC is beginning to look at cross-border infrastructure projects which will promote regional integration. TDA is doing life-cycle cost analysis on government procurement that will well position U.S. goods and services vis-a-vis Chinese competitors because it will emphasize quality and maintenance. And finally, the whole array of core trade and finance and development programs needs to be continued to be supported and backed up. I know this committee has worked very hard, for example, on having foreign commercial service officers throughout the continent. Those officers are setting up in places like Angola and Mozambique as we speak, and this is also very important.

Let me just also underline that Africa is an incredibly important market to General Electric. It is one that we care deeply about, and we look forward to working with this committee and the U.S. Congress and the administration on ways that we can work together to improve energy access, but also ensure sustainability and higher quality of life across the continent.

Thank you very much.

[The prepared statement of Mr. Renigar follows:]

PREPARED STATEMENT OF DEL RENIGAR

Mr. Chairman, Ranking Member Markey, and members of the subcommittee—thank you for the opportunity to testify today on the U.S.-Africa Leaders Summit and the related issue of energy access in Africa. I am Del Renigar, Senior Counsel for Global Government Affairs and Policy, for General Electric.

GE IN AFRICA

GE has a rich history in Africa that spans more than 100 years. GE's capability and global expertise in the power generation, health care, rail transportation, water, oil and gas, and aviation sectors allow us to play a significant role in the development of the continent. We now have more than 2,350 employees across more than 25 countries in the region, providing solutions that support Africa's infrastructure and sustainable growth and increasing U.S. investment and trade with the region.

In addition to the power generation portfolio which I will discuss momentarily, GE provides leading technology and services for the exploration and production of oil and gas, freight locomotives and aircraft engines, and imaging and diagnostic solutions for hospitals and clinics. From Transnet in South Africa to Ethiopian Airlines to hospitals in Kenya, to power projects in Nigeria and oil companies across the continent, Africa is home to some of GE's best customers and most important deals.

Africa has been GE's fastest-growing region since 2000. But lasting growth, both for the continent and for companies that invest there, depends on sustaining investment and fostering partnerships on both sides of the Atlantic. To this end, when President Obama hosted over 40 African heads of state in Washington, DC, for the first-ever U.S.-Africa Leaders Summit, GE sought to maximize this unprecedented gathering of public and private stakeholders.

With more than 30 GE leaders in town for the week-long event, GE teams across three regions (United States, sub-Sahran Africa, and North Africa) partnered to host six major events, including a thought leadership conference with The Economist called Africa Ascending; orchestrated 100+ bilateral meetings with leaders; and announced more than $2 billion in facility development, skills training, and sustainability initiatives across Africa by 2018. Our investment will be focused in three strategic areas: building infrastructure, delivering localized solutions to customers, and capacity-building. Some of the specific new deliverables include:

- Supplying small, distributed gas turbines in Algeria and Nigeria to increase grid reliability;
- Updating and expanding a "Company-to-Country" agreement with Nigeria to support infrastructure projects and the transfer of skills and technology;
- Providing approximately $1 billion in railway and power equipment to Angola;
- Providing approximately $1 billion in rail equipment to South Africa
- Providing approximately $500 million in aircraft engines to Ethiopian Airlines;
- Supporting scholarship programs in Angola and Mozambique;
- Enabling leadership training, technical support, and access to capital for young entrepreneurs as a part of the Young Africa Leaders Initiative (YALI);
- Partnering with the Bush Institute on its Pink Ribbon Red Ribbon initiative, which provides technical assistance and capacity-building related to cancer and HIV/AIDS; and
- Investing $20 million over the next 5 years in health programs across Africa through the GE Foundation to train nurse anesthetists and biomedical equipment technicians.

GE's engagement continues beyond the conclusion of the event itself. In response to an Executive order signed at the summit, Commerce Secretary Pritzker established the President's Advisory Council on Doing Business in Africa to advise the President on strategies for strengthening commercial engagement. Jay Ireland, President and CEO of GE Africa, is honored to serve on the Council, and GE is playing an active role in informing the Council's recommendations on trade and investment, particularly related to infrastructure.

GE believes there is profound opportunity in Africa and that U.S. companies should be aggressively engaging and investing in the continent now to be part of its long-term growth. At the same time, however, there are challenges. Power inefficiencies cost the region $3.2 billion annually in lost productivity, while consumption is only one-tenth of that found elsewhere in the developing world. This means that it takes an Ethiopian 2 years to consume the amount of energy an American or European uses in a matter of days. Without reliable and affordable power, Africa's growth will be constrained, entrepreneurs and small and medium enterprises will not be able to grow, and health care and education will be unable to meet the needs of a rapidly growing population.

African countries can build sustained and inclusive economic growth by increasing access to reliable and affordable power, and many African companies are taking steps to do just that. Afrisol Energy, a 4-year-old Kenyan company, is looking to turn waste into fuel to power Nairobi's slums and rural neighborhoods. The biodigesters it is developing will both alleviate sanitation problems and generate electricity to allow school children to read after dusk or enable clinics to refrigerate vaccines.

Afrisol's work is symbolic of the inventiveness and entrepreneurial spirit that drive people to overcome structural barriers and unlock growth potential. The company was one of the winners of an innovation challenge launched by GE, USAID and the U.S.-Africa Development Foundation that awarded funding to businesses working to bring sustainable, renewable energy technologies to underserved markets. Afrisol was one of more than 150 entries, a fact that illustrates how many African companies are innovating to solve the region's challenges.

Last fall, GE and our partners awarded grants to four Nigerian companies that are working to develop localized biogas facilities, biomass power generation plants, a solar-powered microgrid, and a solar maize-mill processing facility. Eighteen other innovators from Kenya, Ethiopia, Tanzania, Liberia, and Ghana also received $100,000 grants to scale up projects providing renewable solutions to energy challenges in communities outside the national grid.

At GE, we believe these and other distributed power systems can help address the power needs of Africa. Distributed power technologies are small power systems typically ranging in size from 100 kW to 100 MW and located at, or near, the point of use. The current suite of distributed power technologies often includes natural gas and diesel-powered reciprocating engines, small gas turbines, fuel cells, solar panels and wind turbines.

Africa has a unique set of conditions that make distributed power technologies particularly attractive. Distributed power is critical to increasing electrification rates in these areas and providing basic services to these populations.

To be clear, even though the drivers for distributed power are strong today, Africa will still need centralized power and large-scale gas and power grids to accommodate a variety of fuels. Increasing urbanization and the need to capture economies of scale for cities and industrial centers will drive need for central power stations. In our view, the scalability and flexibility of distributed power will complement rather than fully displace centralized power development.

GAS TO POWER

Power is essential to Africa's continued growth, and new energy discoveries are making it possible to address the huge needs of the region. Gas is poised to capture a larger share of the world's energy needs. World gas demand could reach approximately 4,600 BCM by 2025, which is 32 percent higher than today. Regional gas markets are expanding. A global network is developing rapidly, but to capture the efficiency and environmental benefits relative to other hydrocarbons, infrastructure development needs to accelerate, particularly in Africa. Gas will be an attractive alternative to oil in transportation and other distributed energy settings as new supplies are brought online. Further, as regional economies grow, Africa will increasingly look to supply its own agricultural and industrial needs as well as export gas.

Gas-to-power initiatives are a way to make power available to people who need it. Despite the region's gaping power deficit, it is endowed with over 400 trillion cubic feet (Tcf) of gas reserves. Nigeria in particular has among the largest gas reserves in the world (180 Tcf). Tanzania is another example where analysts estimate recent gas finds totaling 25 to 30 Tcf of recoverable resources. These resources have the potential to bring electricity to the 82 percent of the country's population currently without reliable power while transforming Tanzania into a natural gas exporter. Bringing these stranded assets "online" will help meet the urgent demand for electricity and provide an alternative to diesel in low-income countries.

In sub-Saharan Africa, GE sees a tremendous opportunity to work with a broad set of partners to enable reliable, domestic power through gas-to-power projects. The basic concept behind GE's gas-to-power initiative entails convening stakeholders—including governments, developers, fuel suppliers, equipment providers and financiers—to craft a workable, holistic approach to identifying and delivering gas resources to add new power generation capacity where it is needed and makes economic sense. Local needs vary drastically across and even within countries, and each requires a solution tailored to that context.

One of the greatest benefits of these systems is their scalability. The gas-to-power solution can serve distributed power needs as well as those of larger cities or regions. Systems can be designed to address the challenges and demands of specific customers or geographies.

Take Ghana as an example. Since 2012, the country has faced power shortages caused by inadequate and unreliable gas supplies to run power plants. GE is working with a set of partners to develop Ghana 1000, sub-Saharan Africa's largest-integrated gas to power project. The project consists of a floating storage and regasification unit (FSRU), possibly first in-service for sub-Sahara Africa, and related infrastructure for the import and domestic use of liquefied natural gas (LNG). The LNG will be used to power a 1300MW combined cycle power plant, located in Aboadze in the Western Region of Ghana. Beyond the scope of the project itself, the FSRU will have additional capacity to allow other power generators to shift from liquid fuels to LNG for power generation.

This project offers significant economic and environmental benefits. LNG can potentially lower the cost of power in Ghana by up to 35 percent, reducing energy costs by $1 billion annually. Reliable power supplies and LNG imports will drive significant new economic activity, both within Ghana and elsewhere in the region. By shifting up to 3GW of thermal capacity from light crude oil to cleaner natural gas, the project will significantly reduce emissions and deliver associated health and environmental benefits.

At the same time, GE has also made a significant commitment to training and capacity-building in Ghana. In partnership with Ashesi University College, GE is helping develop an academic curriculum to train students in skills needed to thrive in the country's growing energy sector. GE is also providing 4-year scholarships to 100 engineering students in Ghanaian universities and vocational institutions. We believe these investments will help build the workforce needed to ensure and oversee the sustained success of Ghana's energy economy.

When it is complete, the Ghana 1000 project will be a signature accomplishment of the Power Africa Initiative. We are currently working with USAID, OPIC, Ex-Im, and the MCC to ensure a clear federal commitment to the success of the project. Efforts at this scale require a whole-of-government approach, which is embodied in the goals and objectives of Power Africa.

THE OPPORTUNITIES AND CHALLENGES IN NIGERIA

Another key region with huge gas-to-power potential is Nigeria. It is the largest country in Africa and accounts for 47 percent of West Africa's total population, yet less than half of its 179 million people have access to electricity and only 20 percent in rural areas. Despite the fact that Nigeria is the largest oil exporter in Africa and has the largest natural gas reserves in the continent, electricity scarcity is severely constraining economic growth and development.

One of the challenges in the power sector is an underdeveloped domestic gas network and underinvestment in gas production. Despite large gas reserves and by-product gas from its oil production, low fixed prices for gas do not sufficiently incentivize companies to capture this resource. Instead they re-inject the gas to boost oil production or flare it off. Key elements of the Gas Master Plan in Nigeria are advancing and could help—including price adjustments and key infrastructure—but the process has been painfully slow.

In August 2013, Nigeria announced the largest power sector privatization in the world, breaking up the large national power company, selling off of generation assets to private investors, and separating transmission and distribution into separate operating companies. These efforts are starting to yield positive benefits and are attracting foreign and domestic investments in the power sector. Investors and developers, however, are concerned that a number of key representations by the Nigerian Government have not yet been met, specifically the assurance of the gas allocation for the projects and elements of the government support agreements that are essential for investors taking risk in these new private companies.

For example, the Azura project, a 450 MW gas-fired power plant located in Edo State, Nigeria, had been seen as the model for integrated power projects (IPP), however the Nigerian Government has cast doubt as to whether the structure used for Azura will remain the same for new greenfield investments.

As a result of these recent setbacks, we believe the market in Nigeria has slowed and that investors are watching developments to assess the feasibility of the projects and level of Nigerian Government support. Fresh engagement by the U.S. Government to convene investors, developers, and Nigerian Government partners is needed to encourage continued reforms.

FEDERAL POLICY OPPORTUNITIES

The barriers to powering communities and cities across the continent are increasingly becoming less physical, but more procedural. While there is increasing private investment in energy projects in Africa, there is a continued need for active government involvement to keep these significant public-private partnerships on track. We consistently require government engagement in the details, to keep projects on track through implementation and execution. There is an ongoing government role to help solve issues relating to how to agree to contracts more efficiently, how to properly price gas once it is brought to market, and most especially, how to finance energy projects.

It is critical that our customers have access to competitive financing to support these sorts of deals. We support reauthorizing the Overseas Private Investment Corporation (OPIC) and the Export-Import Bank (Ex-Im), and we encourage Congress to seek improvements to make both institutions more flexible and user-friendly, and to use the full range of their tools and authorities. Similarly, it is important to ensure that the U.S. Agency for International Development (USAID) has sufficient funding and flexibility to use its delegated credit authority to work with companies on projects. We also support efforts led by several members of this committee to ensure sufficient Commerce Department resources for commercial, advocacy and market intelligence support in sub-Saharan Africa.

Coupled with these programmatic efforts and ongoing oversight, we encourage Congress to continue to support, expand, and improve the core federal programs that enable U.S. companies to meet the needs of foreign markets. At GE, nearly 60 percent of our revenues derives from markets abroad—up from 40 percent just a decade ago. Much of our opportunity for future growth lies in these expanding markets, and these sales sustain our significant domestic manufacturing base, including thousands of jobs in research, design, engineering, assembly and services.

CONCLUSION

Thank you for the opportunity to share GE's experiences in sub-Saharan Africa. The 2014 U.S.-Africa Leaders Summit helped to further strengthen diplomatic and economic ties between governments and business leaders from both sides. We are having meaningful conversations about sustainable growth models, improving standards of living, reducing wealth disparity, and improving access to energy. Governments, companies and the confluence of public and private capital are all part of an equation in which the whole can be greater than the sum of the parts.

Building on the outcomes of the summit, we look forward to continuing to work with this committee and our partners to support the U.S. Government's ongoing efforts to power economic growth and advance prosperity across the continent.

I am happy to answer any questions you may have. Thank you.

Senator FLAKE. Thank you, Mr. Renigar.

Ms. Tuttle.

STATEMENT OF SUSAN C. TUTTLE, DIRECTOR, MIDDLE EAST AND AFRICA GOVERNMENT AND REGULATORY AFFAIRS, IBM CORPORATION, WASHINGTON, DC

Ms. TUTTLE. Thank you. Good morning, Chairman Flake, Ranking Member Markey, Senator Isakson, and Senator Coons. Thank you very much for the opportunity to share IBM's views on the challenges and opportunities that we see in Africa.

IBM does business in over 170 countries, but several years ago IBM made a decision to significantly expand our investments across the continent. Ginni Rometty, IBM's chairman, president, and CEO, was one of a select few U.S. CEOs to speak at the U.S.-Africa Business Forum, which was a major component of the U.S.-Africa Leaders summit, where she shared IBM's enthusiasm and optimism about the potential of the African economies.

IBM has operated in Africa since 1920 and has had a direct presence there since 1939. In 2006, we had offices in 4 African countries, but today we have a direct presence in 24.

IBM launched its first African research lab in 2013, our 12th global research lab, where researchers are focused on finding solutions to Africa's most pressing challenges in many of the key areas that you highlighted.

It is important to remember that Information and Communication Technology (ICT) is a transformative core enabler that benefits all sectors of the economy, and there is ample cause for optimism that modern technologies and market-based systems will help provide the boost that African countries need to participate fully and successfully in the global community.

Key opportunity areas include banking and financial services, telecommunications, energy and utilities, health care, government, agriculture, retail, and the tech sector. My written testimony includes examples of where IBM is engaging in each of these areas.

IBM is keenly focused on building the skills and capacities of Africa's people and institutions, and has many ambitious and collaborative initiatives involving academia, government, and enterprises. The Young African Leaders Initiative, or the YALI Network, was highlighted during the U.S.-Africa Leaders Summit. IBM is partnering with the U.S. Government, working closely with Notre Dame and Yale, where IBM Fellows are engaging YALI participants on topics ranging from creativity and leadership to business strategy, social technologies, and financing.

IBM also launched several initiatives to help curb the spread of Ebola in West Africa, including a citizen engagement and analytic system in Sierra Leone that enables communities affected by Ebola to communicate their issues and concerns directly to the government. We also donated IBM connections technology to strengthen Nigeria's Lagos state government's preparedness for future disease outbreaks, and most recently provided a global platform for sharing Ebola-related open data.

The U.S.-Africa Leaders Summit sent a strong message to the African leaders about the importance of Africa to the United States and to U.S. companies, but we need sustained focus and engagement in order to see real results. Africa is growing rapidly, but doing business in Africa comes with a unique set of challenges. It is a continent of 54 countries, each with its own political, economic, and cultural dynamics and its own pace of development. The U.S. Government can and should continue to play a role in helping open these markets.

We face strong competition across the continent from our foreign competitors whose governments are playing a very active role in providing financial support and strong advocacy for their businesses. The U.S. Government has a different set of tools that they bring to the table, including Ex-Im, OPIC, USTDA, USAID, and the MCC. Businesses, clients, and governments want and need certainty and predictability to grow their businesses, and these U.S. Government assets need to be reauthorized, funded, expanded, and updated to respond to the needs of today's global economy.

The U.S. Government's focus on helping companies navigate the complexities of doing business in Africa has been invaluable. Budget constraints are a reality, but companies of all sizes are benefitting from the advice, guidance, market insights and help in connecting companies to potential partners and government officials. Moreover, increasingly companies are looking for assistance to help resolve business issues and/or policy advocacy.

As a result, we were very pleased about the Department of Commerce's announcement at the summit that they were opening new offices in Angola, Tanzania, Ethiopia, and Mozambique, while expanding their office in Ghana and also reestablishing a position in the Africa Development Bank, all very important for businesses.

One of the key initiatives resulting from the U.S.-Africa Leaders Summit is the trade facilitation under way with the East African Community (EAC). Success with the EAC could lead to other regional initiatives that would eliminate barriers and harmonize processes among African nations, ultimately making it easier for U.S. companies to do business.

Last month the U.S. Government hosted an East Africa Community Trade Ministerial with the EAC trade ministers, and IBM was one of the companies who represented the business community during the business roundtable where we emphasized the importance of digital trade and raised concerns about a growing trend of protectionist forced localization requirements that act as barriers to trade and investment.

I will not turn to the issue of policy engagement and advocacy because this is an area where we really need your help.

As Africa is becoming more fully integrated into the global economy, governments are wrestling with many of the same policy issues as other governments around the world. How do I attract investment? How do I grow my domestic industry, create jobs, and be globally competitive? How do I improve the skills and talent of my local workforce? And what are the right policies for dealing with issues like privacy and cyber-security?

Governments are looking for models to follow, but we are concerned about a growing trend toward embracing protectionist models, particularly in the area of forced localization or local content requirements; in essence, supporting local industries by discriminating against foreign companies. Forced localization policies are not unique to Africa, but we are seeing a growing trend across the continent.

The global economy cannot function without constant streams of data or information moving across borders. Data is a vital source of innovation and competitive advantage, and restrictions can have a negative impact on companies of every size. The Internet facilitates export of goods and services and enables companies, including small- and medium-sized enterprises, to have access to global supply chains, innovative services at competitive prices and participate in the global economy. More and more services are being delivered over the Internet, and we are seeing an increase in digital trade.

While the U.S. Government has begun to engage on this issue, increased focus and attention is needed lest these protectionist policies spread. The goal of growing domestic industries is very valid, but forced localization and restrictions on cross-border data flows (CBDF) is the wrong approach that could ultimately discourage foreign investment, which is also key to economic growth.

In conclusion, again, the summit provided a very important opportunity to send a message to our African counterparts, our African leaders about the importance that Africa holds for the United States and U.S. companies. But we do need a sustained effort, which is why a hearing today is so important and timely, to continue to keep the energy going and focus on Africa.

In order for U.S. companies to remain competitive, we need the active support and engagement of the U.S. Government leveraging all the tools that we have at our disposal. Market opening initiatives such as trade facilitation, a focus of the U.S.-EAC Cooperation Agreement, can greatly increase the ease of doing business.

And finally, as these markets are maturing, an increased focus and engagement on policy-related advocacy is essential. Forced localization is on the rise around the world and is spreading to the

African Continent. In particular, we need to encourage governments to embrace policies that facilitate digital trade or cross-border data flows and reject digital protectionism. Data localization requirements could ultimately discourage investment and job creation, stifle innovation, and make the local economies less competitive, which is the opposite of the goal.

Thank you again for this opportunity to share IBM's views.

[The prepared statement of Ms. Tuttle follows:]

PREPARED STATEMENT OF SUSAN C. TUTTLE

Good morning, Chairman Flake, Ranking Member Markey and distinguished members of the Africa and Global Health Policy Subcommittee. Thank you for the opportunity to speak with you today and share IBM's views on the opportunities and challenges we see as we aggressively expand our business in Africa.

IBM does business in over 170 countries but several years ago, IBM took a fresh, hard look at what was happening in Africa, beyond the media headlines; and ultimately made a decision to significantly expand our investments across the continent. Ginni Rometty, IBM's Chairman, President, and CEO was one of a select few U.S. CEOs to speak at the U.S.-Africa Business Forum, a major component of the Leaders summit, where she shared IBM's enthusiasm and optimism about the potential for the African economies. We see Africa as a key emerging market of the current economic era, offering major opportunities for growth and transformation across multiple industry sectors.

IBM IN AFRICA

After nearly a century of playing a vital role in Africa's development, IBM is now a part of the continent's technological fabric, business and community. As a technology leader, IBM is helping boost the capabilities of the African people and its institutions—including skills, technology infrastructure, governance, and scientific research.

IBM has operated in Africa since 1920 and has had a direct presence since 1939. In 2006 we had offices in four African countries. IBM has increased its direct presence to 24 countries: South Africa, Nigeria, Mauritius, Ghana, Senegal, Kenya, Tanzania, Morocco, Egypt, Tunisia, Angola, Uganda, Zambia, DR Congo, Sierra Leone, Namibia, Seychelles, Algeria, Malawi, Gabon, Chad, Niger, Burkina Faso, and Madagascar.

IBM launched its first African Research Laboratory in 2013 (12th globally) where researchers are focused on finding solutions to Africa's most pressing challenges across health care, education, water and sanitation, human mobility and agriculture. We're working closely with Africans to identify solutions that are relevant for Africa.

INFORMATION AND COMMUNICATIONS TECHNOLOGY (ICT) OPPORTUNITIES

It's important to remember that Information and Communications Technology (ICT) is a transformative core-enabler that benefits ALL sectors of the economy—from transportation to health care; energy to education; water to public safety; infrastructure to government, etc. There is ample cause for optimism that modern technologies and market-based systems will help to provide the boost that African countries need to participate fully and successfully in the global community. Key opportunity areas include:

Banking and Financial Services.—Nearly every bank in Africa now operates some form of online or mobile banking and with the right solutions, more than 60 percent of Africans could have access to banking services by 2025.

Ghana's Fidelity Bank chose IBM to drive its transformation agenda. IBM is helping bank the unbanked in the Democratic Republic of Congo. Nedbank, based in South Africa, tapped into IBM's Analytics to improve customer experience by leveraging social insights.

Telecommunications.—There were 650 million mobile subscribers in Africa as of 2012, more than Europe or the United States, with many quickly converting to become connected smartphone users.

IBM's African expansion program was accelerated by a deal with Bharti Airtel to create an integrated telecommunications infrastructure throughout

17 countries in sub-Saharan Africa. Surfline Communications in Ghana selected IBM's Cloud solutions to expand its business across West Africa.

Energy and Utilities.—Utilities companies are embarking on large-scale upgrades of aging network infrastructure. From field, to finance, to call centers, IT systems will be integrated for smarter utility operations.

IBM is providing automated systems offering real time status of all business processes for Kenya Power.

Healthcare.—$25–$30 billion is expected to be invested in Africa's Healthcare Infrastructure by the end of 2016. Building sustainable health care systems is one of Africa's greatest health challenges—in some areas, more than 50 percent of the population does not have access to health care.

IBM is working with South Africa's Metropolitan Health to launch the first commercial application of IBM's "Watson" cognitive computing technology in Africa to provide personalized patient care. The Zambian Government and IBM are providing improved access to life saving drugs. Supported by the World Bank, the Department for International Development, UNICEF and London Business School, Zambia's Medical Stores Limited (MSL) will deploy a new medical supply chain pilot project using analytics and mobile technologies to better manage medicine inventory and delivery.

Government.—Significant investments are being made in e-government initiatives (e.g., citizen ids, personal security, and citizen engagement) and modernization of core systems such as taxation and Customs.

South Africa's Gauteng Fire and Disaster Management Center, a provincial public safety authority, has reduced emergency response time from days to hours and gained a comprehensive picture of disaster situations by using IBM's disaster management solutions. IBM and UNICEF in Uganda on U-report, a free SMS-based reporting tool that allows the Ugandan youth to communicate with their government and community leaders using their cell phones.

Agriculture.—Africa has 60 percent of the world's uncultivated arable land, making it a huge potential food source.

With "Project Lucy," IBM researchers in Africa, together with their business and academic partners, are using IBM's 'Watson' and related cognitive technologies to learn and discover insights from Big Data to develop commercially viable solutions to Africa's grand challenges in agriculture, as well as health care, education, water and sanitation, and human mobility. Lucy is the name given to the earliest known human descendant, whose remains were discovered in Africa 400 years ago.

Retail.—90 percent of commerce in Africa is at traditional, informal retailers while malls are limited to a handful of urban areas. Supply chain remains a challenge in Africa, but low rates of formal retail and increasing urbanization demonstrates room for growth.

Kenya's Bidco, a manufacturer and marketer of consumer products, selected an IBM IT solution and services to drive its Africa growth strategy.

Technology Sector and ICT Development.—Africa has a fast-growing information technology market, which according to the World Bank is expected to grow to $150 billion by 2016.

BUILDING SKILLS & CAPABILITIES IN AFRICA

IBM is keenly focused on building the capacities of Africa's people and institutions—including knowledge, technology infrastructure, business sophistication, and governance. IBM has many ambitious initiatives that are collaborative across academia, government, and enterprise; and built into the fabric of the communities and organizations in which we do business. Having a talented and skilled workforce is essential for business because employees are a company's greatest asset.

- The administration's important program, the Young African Leaders Initiative (YALI) Network was also part of the U.S.-Africa Leaders Summit. IBM is partnering with the U.S. Government and working closely with Notre Dame and Yale, where IBM Fellows are engaging YALI participants on topics ranging from creativity and leadership, to business strategy, social technologies, and financing.
- IBM has formed partnerships with several leading University's across Africa in South Africa, Kenya, Mauritius, Ghana, and Nigeria.

- IBM's Leadership Education and Development (LEAD) program brings together MBA students from Africa with faculty and students from leading U.S. universities and IBM executive training.
- IBM runs programs in Africa that help nurture young talent:
  - ○ Accelerating Critical Expertise (ACE), a program designed to accelerate expertise of critical job role pipeline so future leaders are better prepared.
  - ○ Elevate, which is designed to accelerate the professional growth of high-potential women by developing their leadership skills through a customized and tailored learning plan.
  - ○ Leadership Development Roadmap, which helps manager-identified junior talent grow their leadership skills through different learning opportunities.
- IBM developed the Africa Technical Academy program across Africa, which is open to academia, IT specialists and IBM clients. It helps them identify technology solutions to problems facing businesses and the public sector.

IBM'S CORPORATE SOCIAL PROGRAMS IN AFRICA

Corporate Social Responsibility remains a priority for IBM and we've undertaken a number of initiatives across Africa focused on education and skills development, technology solutions, and awarding Smarter Cities Challenge grants to help cities identify solutions to make cities "smarter" and more effective. One of IBM's unique programs is the IBM Corporate Service Corps (CSC) or a corporate version of the "Peace Corps." Through the Corporate Service Corps (CSC), IBM blends social responsibility and business expertise to produce a triple benefit: pro bono problem solving for governments and communities, leadership development for IBM employees, and a greater understanding of new markets for IBM. By the end of 2015, IBM Corporate Service Corps will have dispatched approximately 2,800 IBM employees originating from over 60 countries on engagements to 38 countries. Africa is one of the focal points of the program and to date, the CSC has deployed approximately 800 IBM employees for projects in South Africa, Ethiopia, Angola, Senegal, Tanzania, Nigeria, Ghana, Kenya, Morocco, and Egypt.

IBM'S EFFORTS TO HELP FIGHT EBOLA

IBM launched several initiatives to help curb the spread of Ebola in West Africa. They include a citizen engagement and analytics system in Sierra Leone that enables communities affected by Ebola to communicate their issues and concerns directly to the government; a donation of IBM Connections technology in Nigeria to strengthen the Lagos State government's preparedness for future disease outbreaks; and a global platform for sharing Ebola-related open data.

The efforts combine expertise from IBM's global network of research labs with the company's years of experience in humanitarian disaster response by applying mobile technology, data analytics, and cloud computing to help governments and relief agencies as they seek to contain the deadly disease.

The work benefits from contributions from a number of partners including Sierra Leone's Open Government Initiative, Cambridge University's Africa's Voices project, Airtel and Kenya's Echo Mobile.

U.S. GOVERNMENT'S CRITICAL ROLE

The U.S.-Africa Leaders Summit sent a strong message to the African Leaders of the importance of Africa to the U.S. and U.S. companies; but we need sustained focus and engagement in order to see real results. Africa is growing rapidly but doing business in Africa comes with a unique set of challenges. It's a continent of 54 countries; each with its own political, economic, and cultural dynamics—and its own pace of development. The U.S. Government can and should continue to play a role in helping open these markets.

USG ECONOMIC SUPPORT—LEVERAGING ALL OF OUR TOOLS

We face strong competition across the continent from our foreign competitors whose governments are playing a very active role in providing financial support and strong advocacy to their businesses. The U.S. Government has a different set of tools that they bring to the table, including, EXIM, OPIC, USTDA, USAID, and the Millennium Challenge Corporation (MCC). Businesses, clients, and governments want and need certainty and predictability to grow their businesses; and these USG assets need to be reauthorized, funded, expanded, and updated to respond to the needs of today's global economy.

The U.S. Government's focus on helping companies navigate the complexities of doing business in Africa has been invaluable. Budget constraints are a reality but companies of all sizes are benefitting from the advice, guidance, market insights, and help in connecting companies to potential partners and/or appropriate government officials. Moreover, increasingly, companies are looking for assistance to help resolve business issues and/or policy advocacy. As a result, we were very pleased about the Department of Commerce's announcement at the summit that they were opening new offices in Angola, Tanzania, Ethiopia, and Mozambique, while expanding operations in Ghana and reestablishing a position at the Africa Development Bank.

EAST AFRICA COMMUNITY (EAC) TRADE FACILITATION

One of the key initiatives resulting from the U.S.-Africa Leaders Summit is the trade facilitation effort underway with the East African Community, i.e., Kenya, Tanzania, Rwanda, Uganda, and Burundi. The U.S. and EAC business communities are very engaged and supportive of this effort to remove barriers to trade and more fully integrate the region. Success with the EAC could lead to other regional initiatives that would eliminate barriers and harmonize processes among African nations, ultimately making it easier for U.S. companies to do business. Last month, the U.S. Department of Commerce hosted a U.S.-East Africa Community Trade Ministerial with the EAC Trade Ministers. IBM was one of the three U.S. companies representing the business community during the U.S.–EAC Commercial Dialogue Roundtable where we discussed areas of needed focus and next steps. Progress is being made in some areas such as Customs and agreement was reached to expand the focus to include "Digital Trade" facilitation, among others.

POLICY ENGAGEMENT AND ADVOCACY

We need your help.

As Africa is becoming more fully integrated into the global economy, governments are wrestling with many of the same policy issues as other governments around the world. How to attract investment? How to grow domestic industry and increase exports in order to be globally competitive? How to improve the skills and talent of the local workforce? What are the right policies for dealing with issues such as privacy and cyber security?

Governments are looking for models to follow but we are concerned about a growing trend toward embracing protectionist models, particularly in the area of forced localization or local content requirements. In essence, supporting local industries by discriminating against foreign companies. These policies come in a variety of flavors: from requiring local ownership and management of operations, local employment requirements, mandated technology transfer, local manufacturing and production of inputs and materials—AND restrictions on movement of data across borders. Forced localization policies are not unique to Africa but we are seeing a growing trend in countries like Nigeria, South Africa, Kenya, and most recently in Ghana.

DIGITAL TRADE OR CROSS-BORDER DATA FLOW RESTRICTIONS

The global economy cannot function without constant streams of data or information moving across borders. Data is a vital source of innovation and competitive advantage and restrictions can have a negative impact on companies of every size. The Internet facilitates exports of goods and services and enables companies, including small- and medium-sized enterprises (SMEs) to have access to global supply chains, innovative services at competitive prices and participate in the global economy. Moreover, a wide range of services, including education, financial, business, news, and health, are increasingly being delivered via the Internet, leading to a growth in "Digital Trade." Requirements for in-country processing and storage of data or placing onerous restrictions on transfers of data out of the country are impediments to doing business.

The U.S. Government has begun to engage on this issue but increased focus and attention is needed lest these protectionist policies spread. The goal of growing domestic industries is valid but forced localization is the wrong approach that could ultimately discourage foreign investment, which is also key to economic growth.

CONCLUSION

In summary, the U.S.-Africa Leaders Summit provided a valuable and critical opportunity to reinforce the importance of Africa to the U.S. Government and U.S. companies. There are tremendous potential market opportunities but much progress still needs to be made to improve the ease of doing in a challenging environment. Capitalizing on the momentum created by the summit will require a sustained effort and focus, which makes this hearing both timely and important.

In order for U.S. companies to remain competitive, we need the active support and engagement of the U.S. Government; leveraging all of the tools and assets they bring to the table and working to find new ways of providing assistance.

Market opening initiatives such as the trade facilitation focus of the U.S.–EAC Cooperation Agreement can greatly improve the ease of doing business. The realization of a common market that enables cross-border trade and implements a common set of regulations, procedures, and documentation requirements will create a more transparent and predictable environment—that ultimately will attract more investment.

Finally, as these markets are maturing an increased focus and engagement on policy-related advocacy is essential. Forced localization is on the rise around the world and is spreading to the African Continent. In particular, we need to encourage governments to embrace policies that facilitate Digital Trade or cross-border data flows across the Internet and reject "digital protectionism." Data localization requirements could ultimately discourage investment and job creation, stifle innovation and make the local economies less competitive—which is the opposite of the goal.

Thank you again for this opportunity to share IBM's views.

Senator FLAKE. Thank you, Ms. Tuttle.

Mr. Bollyky.

STATEMENT OF THOMAS J. BOLLYKY, SENIOR FELLOW FOR GLOBAL HEALTH, ECONOMICS, AND DEVELOPMENT, COUNCIL ON FOREIGN RELATIONS, WASHINGTON, DC

Mr. BOLLYKY. Chairman Flake, Ranking Member Markey, Senators Isakson and Coons, I am grateful for the opportunity to testify today about health and private-sector investment in sub-Saharan Africa. It is an honor to be here.

I am going to make three fundamental points: improvements in health in sub-Saharan Africa have been crucial for improved economic performance and investment; second, that there are recent developments that show that those improvements are at risk; and third, that U.S. leadership and contributions from the private sector can do something to address this unfinished health agenda in sub-Saharan Africa.

Over the last decade, U.S. support for better health in sub-Saharan Africa has been strong, it has been bipartisan, and it has been cost-effective. The United States is the leading funder of global health worldwide. That funding has accounted for just two-tenths of U.S. spending, but the returns on that investment in sub-Saharan Africa have been spectacular.

Since the rollout of the PEPFAR program, death and disability from HIV has dropped 17 percent in sub-Saharan Africa. With more support for childhood immunization and maternal and newborn care, infant mortality is down nearly 20 percent in the region over the same period. That means 700,000 children who would have not otherwise reached their fifth birthday are now doing so. That is a tremendous achievement.

Premature death and disability from malaria, TB, and other communicable diseases have also declined.

But the health gains in sub-Saharan Africa are not just humanitarian. A decade ago, Coca-Cola reported routinely hiring two workers for every job opening in sub-Saharan Africa due to the likelihood that one of them would become terminally ill. Now a healthier, more stable labor force is spurring economic growth and investment in the region. A recent Lancet Commission led by former U.S. Treasury Secretary Larry Summers concluded life expectancy gains in sub-Saharan Africa have fueled a nearly 6-percent annual increase in full income between 2000 and 2011. That is the fastest rate of growth in the world on that metric, and that is one reason why U.S. private-sector investments in sub-Saharan Africa over the last decade have been so profitable.

Wealthier sub-Saharan African countries are less aid dependent, they are more stable, and they are better trade and strategic partners for the United States. It is based on that potential that the White House was motivated to hold the first U.S.-Africa Summit last year.

In recent months, however, developments have shown that these health gains are fragile. I will point to two examples. First and, of course, most notably is the Ebola outbreak in West Africa. Prior to the current outbreak, Ebola had killed fewer than 2,000 people in 28 separate outbreaks, all in central Africa, over the 40-year period since the virus was identified in 1976, almost a 40-year period. The current Ebola outbreak has killed five times that number, with enough cases spreading internationally to dominate nightly news and to affect the recent U.S. elections.

What is the difference? With greater trade and travel to, and within, the region, emerging infectious diseases like Ebola are less likely to burn out in rural villages and more likely to reach crowded cities with limited health systems. Sub-Saharan Africa has the fastest rate of urbanization in the world, but it is mostly in small- and medium-sized cities with little public infrastructure.

Ebola is not likely to be the last outbreak in the region, and it has proven expensive already in this particular outbreak. Sierra Leone, Liberia, and Guinea will lose $1.6 billion in economic output in 2015 alone according to the World Bank, which is more than 12 percent of their combined GDP. There are additional costs regionally, as well.

A second example of the health challenges in the region is the stunningly fast increase of heart disease, cancer, and other noncommunicable diseases. A new Council on Foreign Relations task force, cochaired by former Indiana Governor Mitch Daniels and former U.S. National Security Advisor Tom Donilon, found that NCDs are increasing much faster in much younger people with far worse outcomes in sub-Saharan Africa than we have ever seen before.

How fast? Death and disability from NCDs increased 33 percent since 2000 in sub-Saharan Africa, which is more than 200 percent faster than the rate of decline of infectious diseases in that region. These chronic diseases now cause as much death and disability as HIV, malaria, and maternal disorders combined in sub-Saharan Africa. Eighty percent of that burden arises in populations 59 and younger.

The rate of the increase of these diseases is not driven by success. The major drivers of NCDs are the same as the Ebola outbreak. They are limited health systems, persistent poverty, and risk fueled by urbanization and changes in trade, mostly producing pollution, inadequate nutrition, and increased tobacco use.

The good news is that progress on the unfinished health agenda in sub-Saharan Africa is possible. There is a critical need for more investment in public health systems in the region, especially primary care, laboratories, surveillance systems, and critical care facilities. The recent resources that Congress has put forward as part of the Global Health Security Agenda help provide an excellent start.

Despite unhealthier habits, premature death and disability from noncommunicable diseases have declined dramatically in the United States and other high-income countries. Many of the tools and policies that have fueled that decline are cheap, they are effective, but not widely implemented in sub-Saharan Africa. They could be with well-established global health strategies and platforms, and I refer you to the task force report for those strategies.

Finally, the private sector has an important role to play here. The private sector is best suited to invent and adapt technologies for diagnosis, prevention, treatment of both emerging infectious diseases and these non-communicable diseases in low-infrastructure settings. It also has natural concerns and opportunities for improving the health and productivity of their workforces and the size and purchasing power of their consumer base. These concerns played a large role in the international response to HIV.

In conclusion, U.S. and private-sector leadership on health in Africa is important now, as it has been in the past, and for the same reasons. Inclusive economies and investment presuppose healthier and more productive lives.

Thank you very much for your time.

[The prepared statement of Mr. Bollyky follows:]

PREPARED STATEMENT OF THOMAS J. BOLLYKY

Chairman Flake, Ranking Member Markey, and other distinguished members of the subcommittee: I am grateful for this opportunity to testify about global health in sub-Saharan Africa, the progress and setbacks that have occurred in this sector since last year's African Leaders summit, and their implications for private sector-led growth in the region.

Better health has improved the climate for private investment in sub-Saharan Africa, but developments since the African Leaders summit have revealed the fragility of those gains. The prospects for more private sector-led growth in sub-Saharan Africa depend on continued U.S. leadership on global health, especially on emerging infectious diseases, like Ebola, and to address the stunningly fast rise of cancer, diabetes, and cardiovascular and other noncommunicable diseases (NCDs) in the region.

U.S. ROLE IN IMPROVED HEALTH IN SUB-SAHARAN AFRICA

U.S. leadership has played a significant role in improved health in sub-Saharan Africa. A dozen years ago, an HIV/AIDS epidemic that first hit wealthy countries spread the quickest in sub-Saharan Africa, causing large numbers of premature adult deaths and shaking governments. The United States responded. The U.S. President's Emergency Plan for AIDS Relief (PEPFAR) and U.S. support for The Global Fund to Fight AIDS, Tuberculosis, and Malaria delivered lifesaving antiretroviral treatments to millions in the region. The United States expanded its health investments in sub-Saharan Africa in other areas as well, from childhood immunization to nutrition to maternal health. Those investments helped inspire a surge of attention and resources for health in the region from other donors, the private sector, and local governments.

Over the past decade, U.S. support for better health in sub-Saharan Africa has been sustained, bipartisan, and cost-effective. The United States is the leading contributor of global health aid, which accounted for just 0.23 percent of U.S. spending in 2013. The returns on that investment in sub-Saharan Africa, however, have been remarkable.

Since the rollout of the PEPFAR program in 2004, premature death and disability from HIV/AIDS in sub-Saharan Africa have dropped 17 percent.[1] Infant mortality is down nearly 20 percent in the region since 2000, which has meant 700,000 more children now survive their fifth birthday.[2] Premature death and disability from malaria and tuberculosis in sub-Saharan Africa have declined 23 percent and 13 percent, respectively.

The gains from improved health in sub-Saharan Africa have not only been humanitarian, however. A decade ago, Coca-Cola reported routinely hiring two workers for every job opening in sub-Saharan Africa due to the likelihood that one worker might become terminally ill.[3] South African mining companies reported HIV and TB infection rates among their workers that were some of the highest in the world.

A more stable, healthier labor force and an increase in working-age adults due to lower child mortality have spurred economic growth and private investment in sub-Saharan Africa. A recent Lancet commission, led by former U.S. Treasury Secretary, Larry Summers, and the health economist, Dean Jamison, concluded improvements in life expectancy in sub-Saharan Africa between 2000 and 2011 contributed to a nearly 6 percent annual increase in full income, the sum of national income plus the value of the change in mortality (Figure 1). U.S. private-sector investments in sub-Saharan Africa over the past decade have yielded among the highest rates of return of any region in the world.[4]

Contributions of Changes in Life Expectancy to Full Income[5]

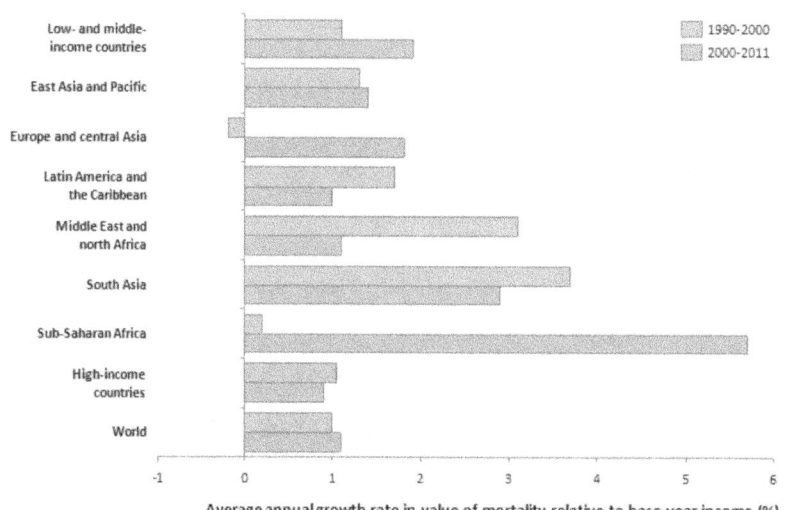

Average annual growth rate in value of mortality relative to base-year income (%)

Adapted from Jamison, Summers, et al., *The Lancet* 382 (2013).

The benefits of continued private investment and economic growth in sub-Saharan Africa would accrue to the United States as well. Wealthier sub-Saharan African countries are less U.S.-aid dependent, more stable, and better trade and strategic partners. As personal incomes grow, many of these countries' demand for exports will rise and begin to shift to the categories in which the United States leads the world: civilian aircraft, pharmaceuticals, machinery and equipment, high-value foods, and entertainment.

The improved economic and strategic prospects in the region encouraged the White House to hold the first ever U.S.-Africa summit in August 2014. The summit offered the opportunity not only to expand on health gains, but also encourage more private investment in energy and infrastructure and forge closer diplomatic ties.

The health initiatives announced at the Leaders summit included: a PEPFAR and Children's Investment Fund Foundation partnership to prevent mother to child transmission of HIV; a U.S.-African private sector initiative on food security and nutrition; and a PEPFAR/Pink Ribbon Red Ribbon initiative on cervical cancer screening in Ethiopia and Namibia, supported by General Electric, GlaxoSmith-Kline, and others.

HEALTH IN SUB-SAHARAN AFRICA SINCE THE LEADERS SUMMIT

In months after the summit, it has become clear that new health challenges are emerging in sub-Saharan Africa. The region has one of the fastest rates of urbanization in the world. Most of that growth is in small- and medium-sized cities with limited public health infrastructure.[6] Inter- and intra-country trade in the region is increasing, but its oversight lags behind. Many sub-Saharan countries lack the basic consumer protections and public health rules that have been in place in most high-income countries for decades.

Life expectancies have improved in sub-Saharan Africa, but without the same gains in personal income and health systems that accompanied longevity in wealthier countries. The median GDP per capita in OECD countries was $4,376 when they achieved a median life expectancy of 60 years in 1947. Sub-Saharan African nations just reached that life expectancy in 2011 and their median GDP per capita was $1,658.[7] The health systems in most sub-Saharan African countries are still built for acute care, not chronic or preventative care. Health spending has increased in recent years, but remains low relative to high-income countries.[8] All the governments in sub-Saharan Africa together spend roughly as much on health annually ($33 billion) as the Government of Poland ($31 billion).[9]

Two developments in the months since the African Leaders Summit demonstrate the health consequences of these trends and the fragility of the recent gains in sub-Saharan Africa.

The most high profile example is the Ebola outbreak in West Africa, which began before the African Leaders summit, but accelerated thereafter. Prior to the current epidemic, Ebola had killed fewer than 2,000 people in 28 outbreaks since the virus was first identified in 1976, all in Central Africa. Ebola has killed nearly five times that number in the last 14 months, with enough cases spreading internationally to dominate nightly news broadcasts and affect recent U.S. elections. The difference? With greater trade and travel to, and within the region, emerging infectious diseases like Ebola are less likely to burn out in rural villages and more likely to reach the crowded cities with limited health systems that are the ideal incubators for outbreaks. The Ebola outbreak may be just a preview of pandemics to come in sub-Saharan Africa.

Through the combined efforts of the local and international responders, the Centers for Disease Control and Prevention and other U.S. agencies, donors, and intergovernmental institutions, new Ebola cases appear finally to be dwindling. The economic cost, however, remains. The most recent World Bank estimates are that Sierra Leone, Liberia, and Guinea will lose $1.6 billion in economic output in 2015 alone, more than 12 percent of their combined GDP. The Ebola outbreak's projected 2015 economic costs in other sub-Saharan African countries is just over half a billion dollars, to be experienced mostly in West Africa.[10]

A second example of changing global health needs is the stunningly fast increase of heart disease, cancers, and other NCDs in sub-Saharan Africa. Once thought to be challenges for affluent countries alone, these diseases have quickly become a leading health concern in sub-Saharan Africa, causing as much death and disability in the region as HIV/AIDS, malaria, and maternal disorders combined.

A new Council on Foreign Relations (CFR)-sponsored Independent Task Force report, cochaired by former Indiana Governor Mitch Daniels and former U.S. National Security Advisor Tom Donilon, found that NCDs are increasing in sub-Saharan Africa faster, in younger people, and with worse outcomes than in wealthier countries.[11] Citing data from the Institute for Health Metrics and Evaluation's groundbreaking Global Burden of Disease project, the Task Force showed that NCD death and disability increased 33 percent between 2000 and 2013, more than 200 percent faster than the decline of infectious diseases in the region, The increase of death and disability of breast cancer and diabetes in the region exceeded 80 percent over the last two decades. More than 80 percent of the NCD burden in sub-Saharan Africa arises in people 59 years of age or younger.

Rates of the most unhealthy behaviors associated with NCDs remain low in sub-Saharan Africa. U.S. adult obesity is more than four times higher than it is in sub-Saharan Africa.[12] The major drivers of these diseases in this region are the same as in the Ebola outbreak: limited health systems, persistent poverty, and risks fueled by urbanization and changes in trade. Inhabitants of densely packed urban areas often face pollution outdoors and the burning of fuels indoors, are more likely to buy tobacco products, and less likely to have access to adequate nutrition. With little access to preventative care and more exposure to these health risks, working-age people in sub-Saharan Africa are more likely to develop an NCD. Without access to chronic care and limited household resources to pay for medical treatment, these people are more likely to become disabled and die young as a result.

The Task Force found that, unless urgent action is taken on NCDs, the economic consequences in sub-Saharan Africa will be significant. Most NCDs are chronic, as is the case with HIV/AIDS. As more patients get sick from NCDs, suffer longer, require more medical care, and die young, the results reverberate. At the household level, it means less income and catastrophic health expenditures. At the national level, it means lower productivity and competitiveness, and a potential missed opportunity to capitalize on the demographic dividend that lifted the fortunes of many higher income countries. At the global level, the World Economic Forum projects that the NCD epidemic will inflict $21.4 trillion in losses in developing countries over the next two decades—a cost nearly equal to the total aggregate economic output ($24.4 trillion) of these countries in 2013. These economic costs will undercut potential U.S. trade partners and allies and undermine existing U.S. and private sector investments in sub-Saharan Africa.

THE UNFINISHED HEALTH AGENDA IN SUB-SAHARAN AFRICA

Progress on the unfinished health agenda in sub-Saharan Africa is possible. The Global Health Security Agenda and the recent resources that Congress has devoted to it provide an excellent start.

There is a critical need to invest in basic public health systems in the region, especially primary health care facilities, laboratories, surveillance systems, and critical care facilities. The use of these systems should not be limited to disease-specific goals, but be responsive to local needs. The public health surveillance and response must be used regularly for routine matters in order to be efficiently scaled in the extraordinary circumstances of an outbreak.

Strengthening health care systems improves our ability to deal with emerging infectious diseases, but also provides a platform for the preventative and chronic care desperately needed for NCDs. Without better functioning health systems, it will be very hard for sub-Saharan Africa to end the cycle of disease and poverty and promote private sector-led growth.

Despite much higher rates of obesity and physical inactivity, premature death and disability from NCDs has declined dramatically in the United States and other high income countries. The reason? Mostly cheap and effective prevention, management, and treatment tools and policies that are not widely implemented in sub-Saharan Africa, but could be with well-established global health strategies. These include low-cost drugs to reduce heart attacks, vaccines to prevent cervical cancer, and providing countries with the opportunity to implement the same tobacco taxes and advertising rules that dramatically cut smoking rates in the United States. Pilot programs can and have integrated these tools and policies into donor-funded programs on HIV/AIDS and other public health system platforms in the region.

The private sector has a twofold role on unfinished health agenda in sub-Saharan Africa. First, the private sector is best suited to invent and adapt technologies for diagnosis, prevention, and treatment of emerging infectious diseases and NCDs in low-infrastructure settings. Second, companies have natural concerns for maintaining the health and productivity of their workforces and the size and purchasing power of their customer base. Large employers were essential to rally global support for addressing HIV/AIDS in the region. They are also at the forefront of designing and implementing innovative health promotion programs for their employees that emphasize exercise, preventative care, better diets, and reduced smoking.

The hard work and generosity of the United States, the private sector, and other donors have helped reduce the plagues, parasites, and blights that have long undercut economic opportunity and investment in sub-Saharan Africa. Extending those initiatives to NCDs and emerging infectious diseases would lessen their worst effects and provide national governments with the time and technical assistance needed to tackle these new threats sustainably on their own. Continued U.S. and private sector leadership on the unfinished health agenda in Africa is as important now as it has been in the past and for the same reasons: a peaceful, inclusive economy presupposes healthier, more productive lives.

End Notes

[1] Murray, Christopher JL, Katrina F. Ortblad, Caterina Guinovart, Stephen S. Lim, Timothy M. Wolock, D. Allen Roberts, Emily A. Dansereau et al. "Global, regional, and national incidence and mortality for HIV, tuberculosis, and malaria during 1990–2013: a systematic analysis for the Global Burden of Disease Study 2013." The Lancet 384, no. 9947 (2014): 1005–1070.

[2] Wang, Haidong, Chelsea A. Liddell, Matthew M. Coates, Meghan D. Mooney, Carly E. Levitz, Austin E. Schumacher, Henry Apfel et al. "Global, regional, and national levels of neonatal, infant, and under-5 mortality during 1990–2013: a systematic analysis for the Global Burden of Disease Study 2013." The Lancet 384, no. 9947 (2014): 957–979.

[3] Krisi Heim, "Corporations Invest in Global Health," Seattle Times, November 11, 2010.

[4] Sveinung Fjose, Leo A. Grünfeld, and Chris Green, "SMEs and growth in Sub-Saharan Africa," MENON Business Economics, June 2010.

[5] Adapted from Dean T. Jamison, Lawrence H. Summers, George Alleyne, Kenneth J. Arrow, Seth Berkley, Agnes Bingawaho, Flavia Bustreo, et al., "Global health 2035: a world converging within a generation," The Lancet 382 (2013): 1898–955, doi:10.1016/S0140–6736(13)62105–4.

[6] Julie E. Fischer and Rebecca Katz, "The International Flow of Risk: The Governance of Health in an Urbanizing World," Global Health Governance 4 (2011); Campbell et al., "Emerging Disease Burdens," i59.

[7] Council on Foreign Relations, Noncommunicable Disease Interactive, available at http://www.cfr.org/diseases-noncommunicable/NCDs-interactive/p33802.

[8] Institute for Health Metrics and Evaluation, "Financing Global Health 2013: Transition in an Age of Austerity," Institute for Health Metrics and Evaluation, 2014, 61–62.

[9] OECD Health Stats: Public Health Expenditure since 2000, via Organization for Economic Co-operation and Development.

[10] World Bank, The Economic Impact of Ebola on Sub-Saharan Africa: Updated Estimates for 2015 (Jan. 20, 2015).

[11] Thomas J. Bollyky, Mitchell E. Daniels, and Thomas E. Donilon. The emerging global health crisis: noncommunicable diseases in low- and middle-income countries. New York, NY: Council on Foreign Relations, 2014. Print.

[12] Ng, Marie, Tom Fleming, Margaret Robinson, Blake Thomson, Nicholas Graetz, Christopher Margono, Erin C. Mullany et al. "Global, regional, and national prevalence of overweight and obesity in children and adults during 1980–2013: a systematic analysis for the Global Burden of Disease Study 2013." The Lancet 384, no. 9945 (2014): 766–781.

Senator FLAKE. Thank you, Mr. Bollyky.

I thank all of you for your testimony, and we will start a round of questions, Mr. Leo first.

You mentioned in your testimony that OPIC needs some serious reforms, and one of the problems that constrains its activity, according to your testimony, is that we have the carbon emissions cap. You say that has effectively pushed the agency out of all natural gas projects in the world's poorest countries.

I met with OPIC officials a few days ago in my office. They claim that the regulations that they have and the carbon cap that has been dealt with in appropriations bills here is not a constraint on their activities. Can you tell me how it is and what we ought to do in Congress to remedy that?

Mr. LEO. Thank you. It is an excellent question. I think it is a question that has a lot of strategic importance as well.

I think one of the central issues on the impact of the carbon cap is around predictability. If we look at power projects anywhere in the world, but particularly in Africa that have a development lifecycle of several years—3, 5, 7 years, depending on the country, depending on the context—the approaches that U.S. investors or private companies will take will be impacted upon predictability.

So I think what we have found in the last several years, particularly since the cap was put in place, is that companies stopped going to seek support from the Overseas Private Investment Corporation because they were not sure if it was going to be in a position to help, and particularly now where you have a cap that is dealt with on a year-by-year basis, that is still a high-risk venture for many companies. If they think about getting far into the stage, having a significant percentage of their project capital evaporate in the middle of a deal, it could be catastrophic when they have already had legal expenses and a number of other things that have gone in. So I think predictability and certainty is a very big issue.

Now, having said that, since the cap was temporarily lifted, my impression talking with a range of different power developers, and

34

there are not that many of them that are engaged that are American, they have increasingly gone to OPIC seeking support and help of a varied nature, whether it is insurance or investment or loans, et cetera. I have been told that the list of projects that OPIC is currently looking at that are of a natural gas nature is actually quite long.

Some of these are very large, like a couple of projects in Nigeria. Some of the Ghana projects were brought up earlier. The scale, if the carbon cap was reintroduced, would absolutely blow what OPIC is able to do in a single project. I mean, basically, historically, they have been able to do one medium-sized gas-fired plant globally per year, and the scale of the need, the scale of the demand just far, far, far exceeds that.

Senator FLAKE. Thank you.

Mr. Renigar, you talked about in Africa, obviously with the telecommunications, many countries have been able to leap frog some of the technology, and some of that is possible in the energy sector. But you mentioned in your testimony that there are constraints there, that that only goes so far. Do you want to elaborate a little on that? What benefit is there to renewables, but where are the limits as well?

Mr. RENIGAR. Absolutely. Thank you, Senator. We agree that renewables do have a role to play in sub-Saharan Africa, as well as distributed power solutions. The reality is, though, when you have a continent that is surrounded by 400 trillion cubic feet of gas, that gas ought to be deployed because gas, in fact, is a clean fuel. That gas can displace diesel and other dirtier fuels. And also gas, because it can be brought on relatively quickly with these gas-to-power projects, has the ability to address the energy access issues relatively quickly.

You also need base load power. Wind, solar, distributed power, biomass, all of these are technologies that can and should be deployed. What we see is a portfolio of technologies to address the massive need for more energy in sub-Saharan Africa.

But given the resources that they have, given the needs for base load power to create stability on the grid, because the wind does not always blow, the sun does not always shine, there is not always biomass nearby. Also, the challenge of having the fuel source and the power within proximity to where the need is, is another challenge that has to be managed.

So gas will always play a significant role in sub-Saharan Africa for the foreseeable future, and it has to be the central point of departure for addressing the need and then use the other technologies where they are needed to do it for smaller scale or for smaller needs or for individual industrial applications.

Senator FLAKE. Thank you.

Ms. Tuttle, you spent a lot of time in your testimony talking about the growing trend of protectionism. You mentioned the need for us to address it here, or government to government. What is the private sector doing in that regard, or how are you trying—what is IBM doing and other companies? Are you trying to remedy these situations on your own, and is there not a need for us to step in at this point? Is it getting that bad?

Ms. TUTTLE. Yes. Thank you, Senator. IBM and members of the business community have been working hard to highlight these issues. As I said in my testimony, forced localization is not an issue that is unique to Africa. These protectionist policies are on the rise all around the world including in countries such as China, India, Brazil, Argentina and Vietnam. And these bad policies are spreading to the African continent as the governments look to replicate what other developing countries are doing.

U.S. companies, we have been talking to Congress about this issue for several years. We have also been reaching out to the administration, including the President and USTR encouraging them to include language in trade agreements to try to address this concern.

The 2014 Trade Promotion Authority legislation also included excellent language to guard against some of the protectionist policies that we are seeing, and we are looking to have that language included in the spring version of the bill that is coming up.

We are doing a whole host of things. Locally, we are engaging with the governments on a one-on-one basis and as a community, to raise concerns as both local companies and foreign investors. We've continued to point out that if these policies spread, their own companies will encounter barriers and will not be able to export their products and services to other markets.

We are encouraging them strongly to look at other options, and that is where, again, the U.S. Government can help. Often it takes a three-pronged approach to resolve issues, i.e., carrot, stick, and a win-win scenario. We have an opportunity with the positive U.S.-Africa engagement established by the summit to try to focus more on the win-win, use less of the stick, and obviously identify possible incentives.

But a more concerted and focused effort is needed. Nigeria is the largest economy on the African continent, and they have a very aggressive—frankly, the worst we've seen—local content policy impacting ICT. The danger is that if these policies succeed in Nigeria, it could spread quickly across the continent. Our concerns are real.

We see an opportunity for the U.S. Government to lean forward and to get more engaged and to help resolve the issue.

Senator FLAKE. Thank you.

Mr. Markey.

Senator MARKEY. Thank you, Mr. Chairman.

Mr. Bollyky, your report is quite startling, that heart disease and cancer is now the global health crisis in Africa, surpassing HIV, malaria, maternal disorders combined. That is where the death rate is. That is what is causing a lot of problems in the country, on the continent.

So what can the United States do in partnering with the private sector in order to deal with this issue, to play a larger role to help Africa with this issue?

Mr. BOLLYKY. Thank you, Ranking Member, for the great question. The long-term solution to chronic diseases in sub-Saharan Africa is the same as it is here in the United States. It is functional health systems. It is more sensible agricultural policies. It is better urban design.

But the fact that sub-Saharan African countries have this long-term task ahead of them on NCDs in doing what we have largely done or have started to do over decades should not distort from the fact that there is much that can be done on NCDs in these countries in the short term. Nobody waited for functional health systems to intervene on HIV in sub-Saharan Africa. If there were shovel-ready health interventions that could be pursued now, we pursued them where they could save people's lives.

The CFR task force report suggested three areas where we have made tremendous progress, and that could be extended to sub-Saharan African countries for cheap. The first basket, again, are the shovel-ready interventions. Here I would put in low-cost care for hypertension, cardiovascular disease, and tobacco control. Cardiovascular disease, premature deaths from cardiovascular disease in the United States have dropped over 40 percent in the last 20 years. It is mostly products, generic drugs, beta blockers, statins that could easily be extended in poorer countries using existing platforms.

Vaccinations for cervical cancer and hepatitis B, which causes liver cancer, something again that can be done internationally through existing delivery platforms at a reasonable cost.

Tobacco control. Every state in the United States has tobacco taxes and restrictions on tobacco advertising. This is largely not the case in sub-Saharan Africa, and there are indications that these countries are increasingly being targeted for expanding the market in that setting.

The second basket of interventions—and this is particularly a role for the private sector—is adapting existing technologies that have made good progress on cancers in high-income settings but have not been extended to lower-income settings. Breast cancer has increased over 100 percent in the last two decades in sub-Saharan Africa. Biopsies and mammography tools are largely unavailable in many of these countries and not usable in low-resource settings but that could be changed with U.S. support.

Diabetes treatment falls in this second category as well.

The third area that was put forward in the task force report is there is a real opportunity for the United States and low- and middle-income countries in sub-Saharan Africa to learn from one another on addressing this NCD challenge moving forward. We are certainly not perfect. We have much higher rates for risk factors for NCDs than these countries do. The obesity rate in the United States is four times higher than it is in sub-Saharan Africa.

Better approaches on population-based prevention and lower-cost chronic care can really do a great deal of good in both settings, and it is an opportunity to work together.

Senator MARKEY. Okay, thank you so much.

Mr. Renigar, can you talk a little bit about corruption in the energy sector in sub-Saharan Africa and what your view is with regard to whether or not actions taken against it are improving or worsening?

Mr. RENIGAR. Thank you, Senator. It is a very good question, and I think when we are talking about doing business in Africa, this is one of the central points that has to be addressed, particularly for American companies going into sub-Saharan Africa.

Senator MARKEY. In the energy sector in particular.

Mr. RENIGAR. Yes, in the energy sector in particular. Our experience has been relatively good in this area because we have the ability to do what I would call more of a top-down approach. So a lot of the projects that we are involved in, we put them in the context of broader GE engagement in the particular country.

So Nigeria, for example, which is one of the countries that people tend to talk about most, we have put in place what we call a company-to-country agreement or MOU between GE and the government of Nigeria where we lay out our strategic priorities across a number of areas. Energy, of course, is one of them. We use this as a mechanism to consult regularly with the President and his ministers on our key projects.

Senator MARKEY. So do you tie your investment strategy to saying you do not want to be involved in activities that have corruption? Is that the understanding that you have as GE goes into a country?

Mr. RENIGAR. Absolutely, and we use the flexibility and availability of our dialogues with their ministers and their leadership to always drive home that we are there to do business and to do it in the right way, and it gives us the mechanism to bring up any issues that come up.

I think what happens is the bureaucracy at lower down levels know that when they are dealing with an American company that regularly talks with the government, they cannot make those kinds of requests.

What I would add, Senator, is that I think one of the ways that we can best get at this corruption is to use the tools of better government procurement policy, better customs policy, better trade facilitation, because a lot of the corruption——

Senator MARKEY. So let me just go to that. So with regard to Power Africa, for example, how can we use that to leverage U.S. investment in the energy sector as a way of extracting anticorruption protections built around those programs? How can we do that?

Mr. RENIGAR. Well, I think there are a number of things that we do. First, when you are doing a Power Africa project, you will also often be getting advocacy from the Commerce Department. The Commerce Department has an anticorruption clause in their advocacy work that you and all of the people on the project have to certify that there is no corruption in the project. So that gives you the certification and the hook.

The other thing that Power Africa is doing is putting advisors embedded in the ministries who can help the bureaucracy work through projects, doing it the right way.

The final point is once you shine the bright light of Power Africa or the bright light of a U.S. company or a U.S. Government interest on a project, it sanitizes it to a certain extent.

Senator MARKEY. And I think that is very important because that gives us a reach into these countries, into the governments who would want an expanded role for the U.S. Government in this investment sector. So the more we do it, the more leverage we have in rooting out the corruption or putting in place a regime that re-

duces corruption in the energy sector in that country. Is that what
you are saying?

Mr. RENIGAR. Absolutely.

Senator MARKEY. Okay, thank you.

Thank you, Mr. Chairman.

Senator FLAKE. Senator Isakson.

Senator ISAKSON. Thank you, Mr. Chairman.

Senator Markey quoted Robert Kennedy's famous quote about Africa years ago. There is another quote that he made in Africa where they had a famine where he said, "Sometimes people see things as they are and ask why. I see things as they never were and ask why not."

I think Africa is at a "why not" point. Africa is at a point where it can grow and become a major factor economically as a trade partner with the United States, as well as a political power with the United States.

But there are three things you all have mentioned that I see are impediments. One is corruption, one is forced localization, and one is the lack of reliable energy that could have jobs and manufacturing for the African people.

Mr. Renigar answered the corruption question for GE.

Ms. Tuttle, IBM's investments, have you run into corruption problems in Africa? Or what do you do to address the potential of corruption?

Ms. TUTTLE. Thank you, Senator. IBM has a very, very robust policy against corruption. We have an annual global training for each one of our employees to reinforce our anti-corruption policies as part of our business conduct guidelines Our employees are required to certify that they understand and will comply with these policies.

I will tell you, too, that we put specific focus, as we were going into the region, on ethics training, and a major part of our company in our trust and compliance focuses within the legal function that does regular training multiple times a year in ensuring that our employees themselves are aware of the pitfalls, the dangers, and avoiding any engagement with corruption.

I will say, too, that Del was just making a very important point, and that is, again, there is always going to be some demand, but it is lessening over time. As the government officials, as they are dealing more and more with U.S. companies, they know that these companies are bound by the Foreign Corrupt Practices Act, and we are seeing a lessening at least of the corruption that we are encountering with the businesses.

So it is important, too, just as you all were touting, U.S. companies are not engaging, we are in a campaign against corruption, and when you are doing business with U.S. companies, the governments are increasingly aware of that fact.

Senator ISAKSON. Thank you very much to both of you.

Ms. TUTTLE. Thank you.

Senator ISAKSON. Thank you for your investment in the continent of Africa.

Mr. Leo, in your testimony, you talked about the Congress should modernize the U.S. development finance tools by creating a modern

U.S. development finance corporation and by making modest reforms to OPIC.

On those modest reforms, I had a visit from OPIC officials the other day, and they talked about going into the equity business. Are you familiar with that? Is that one of the modest reforms you are talking about?

Mr. LEO. In terms of the reforms, I think they largely focus around making sure that U.S. development finance tools reflect the needs in current market dynamics, both for promoting U.S. investors but also for advancing U.S. development policy abroad. And in that context, where OPIC finds itself right now is that they have very limited tools. They can do a couple of things. A number of the other tools, frankly, including equity authority, is housed elsewhere in the government. So USAID has that authority right now. Feasibility studies are at a different agency. Other types of technical assistance are spread across half a dozen different agencies. They are not housed under one roof that is able to bring them all together in a seamless way and in an effective, efficient, and highly accountable way.

So equity, I think, should have consideration. I realize there are strong views for and against it. I think there are lessons from other peer institutions, particularly European institutions, that have used it in a limited way and in an impactful way for development priorities and development outcomes. But like I said, it already exists and is being used.

Senator ISAKSON. In other areas.

Mr. LEO. But it is by USAID. It is in a disjointed way compared to OPIC.

Senator ISAKSON. Ms. Tuttle, I appreciate you mentioning forced localization. Senator Coons and I are dealing with an issue regarding poultry, which is certainly not high-tech but it is certainly a major trade item for Georgia and Delaware. And forced localization in South Africa has kind of caused some barriers to chickens from Delaware and Georgia getting into South Africa.

Is the same thing true with technology? Are they trying to force local use of technology in development to keep people like IBM out?

Ms. TUTTLE. Yes. I mean, I think in many of the countries we started seeing it manifested in the petroleum industry, where we started seeing some forced localization. Then the ITC sector in particular, we are starting to see again—they see it as a growth engine for their economies, so they are starting to target that this is a way we can bring our local domestic industry up and reduce our dependencies on imports.

So, yes, we are starting to see it more and more. But I think the important thing—and this was the point I made in my testimony about how IT has an impact across all sectors. When we were speaking with a Nigerian official, someone from Citibank said you must understand, more and more of their services are being delivered across border. So if you are impeding IBM's ability to move the data and they are a service provider to me, that also impacts my ability to move information across border.

But we are seeing this in everything from local manufacturing, local employment quotas, local product development, local IP, technology transfer. Yes, it is important that companies work together, and, to be honest, in many ways we are already doing many things. We have business partners. We work with local entrepreneurs. Businesses are doing so many things, and the question is what is the negative impact of forcing companies to do things, give up their intellectual property and all of their technologies in order to help build the domestic industry, while keeping us out creates tremendous problems and potential for U.S. companies as we are investing. And as I said, not just U.S. companies but their own companies.

Are there other alternatives to growing and spurring innovation and spurring the domestic growth of their local companies? I think there are.

Senator ISAKSON. Well, my time is up, but I have got to ask you a kind of yes-or-no question. You mentioned Nigeria and Ebola and the role that IBM played in terms of communicating data, if I am not mistaken.

Ms. TUTTLE. Yes.

Senator ISAKSON. Nigeria was the one African country that actually stopped and contained the outbreak. Was that in part due to the communication of data?

Ms. TUTTLE. In the case of Nigeria, they declared victory over the immediate crisis, while we were engaging with the government but at any point in time, the Ebola crisis could suddenly occur again. So thinking about how do we look forward in the future of Ebola and how are we going to deal with it in anticipation that it could arise someplace else I think is an important consideration to have.

Senator ISAKSON. Thanks to all the panelists.

Ms. TUTTLE. Thank you.

Senator FLAKE. Senator Coons.

Senator COONS. Thank you, Chairman Flake and Ranking Member Markey, and to our witnesses for today's important conversation about how we continue to make progress after the U.S.-Africa Leaders Summit of last August. I appreciate the contributions all of you have made to growing the U.S.-Africa relationship and commenting on it.

Mr. Bollyky's testimony and the conversation Senator Isakson just had with Ms. Tuttle about Ebola is a reminder that the legacy of PEPFAR and a lot of our investment in modernizing health care systems in some countries like Nigeria show a very different outcome than we saw in Guinea, Sierra Leone, and Liberia, and there is reason for us to continue to invest in preventive systems, in changing the ground game in terms of health care. I found your testimony particularly interesting in terms of the challenge of what we do next.

But let me turn, if I might, Ms. Tuttle, to your testimony on the opportunities and the tools that we have in the U.S. Government. You commented that Ex-Im, OPIC, USTDA, USAID, MCC, these are the tools in the toolkit; that businesses, clients and governments want and need certainty and predictability to grow their businesses. These U.S. assets need to be reauthorized, funded, expanded and updated to meet the needs of today's global economy.

I would just be interested in each of you briefly commenting, in your experience with GE, your views on whether this is sufficient, or bilateral investment treaties is where we need to go, and how this would contribute to health care modernization. If just each of you would briefly address what is the most important thing we need to do. Is it simply reauthorize and fund, or is there one significant change you would recommend we make to this toolkit?

Ms. Tuttle, if you would start.

Ms. TUTTLE. Ben made a comment about consolidating U.S. Government resources, and we should take a fresh look at what the best approach should be. Each of these organizations and functions have a different mission, a different focus. It takes a long time to figure out how they work, understand the complexity of their processes, how best to engage—and all of this takes time.

There is a lot of pressure to move quickly in these markets and funding requirements are immediate. In fact, African nations have raised concerns about the ability for the U.S. Government to respond quickly with the various programs and tools they offer.

So I think a fresh look at consolidating these organizations would be in order.

I would also say that in some instances, you know we operate in a global economy, and of course it has to benefit the United States, and I appreciate that. But in many instances, the mandates that were developed for these aid agencies and assistance agencies were looking more at movement of goods over borders. More and more services are delivered—we are talking about global Internet, global delivery of services and access to these markets.

So when I think about updating these policies, Ex-Im has made some progress in changing its policies to address the delivery of services, but we need to take a fresh look across all of the programs and ask ourselves what does today's world look like, and how do we update their mandates to be responsive to today's realities and the needs of the companies operating in a global market?

Senator COONS. Let me ask you and Mr. Renigar just a simple yes or no question on this. Because several of these entities are on track now to go away—their authorization is either expiring or expired—it is uncertain whether they will be funded. If they disappeared, would private-sector mechanisms replace them, or are they essential to your continued growth across the continent?

Ms. TUTTLE. I think in many ways they are essential.

Senator COONS. Mr. Renigar.

Mr. RENIGAR. They are essential, Senator, and it would have an adverse impact on our ability to do business in Africa and our ability to compete with China and other competitors, Japan as well, if these tools go away.

I would echo the comments that we need to consolidate them. I think the special sauce of Power Africa has been the whole-of-government approach. China and Japan come in and say we will deliver the solution. We come in and say go talk to MCC, then go talk to TDA, then go talk to USAID. It is confusing. We need the one-stop shop approach.

The other point I would also emphasize is cross-border and regional integration. The reality is in order to strengthen the entire system in sub-Saharan Africa, you need to create scale. And the way to create scale is to do cross-border infrastructure and regional integration.

So make it a one-stop shop, and make it more focused on regional integration and cross-border infrastructure, and I think we could really seize a lot of these opportunities better.

Senator COONS. So absolutely essential, streamline, coordinate, and empower regional.

Mr. Leo.

Mr. LEO. Thank you. I would just reemphasize the need for consolidation and scale. So I think this is a consistent theme that you are hearing. I think the impetus for it stands on its own merit in terms of the potential role and impact for supporting growth opportunities, stability in this increasingly important region.

But particularly when you look at what other nations are already doing, they have already moved to scale. They have already consolidated their tools. The Europeans have done this over a process of decades. The new institutions that have been launched by emerging market nations like China, India, Malaysia, Brazil, they are housed under one roof primarily, and they are at scale. So I think that is what we need to do.

Two quick piecemeal things. If we were not going at consolidation and scale, I would do a couple of things at OPIC. One, I would look at the admin budget. They have an underutilized capital base right now because they do not have enough people to do deals in a rigorous way. And then I would implement a couple of reforms around transparency, tracking impact and publicly reporting it, and making sure that there is explicit criteria that they only do deals that are purely additional. And then bilateral investment treaties. It is a highly underutilized tool.

Senator COONS. Senator Isakson and I are eager to move the African Growth and Opportunity forward but recognize that that is simply extending the current relationship.

My last question would be briefly to you. Why are there not more bilateral investment treaties between the United States and Africa when our European competitors or Asian competitors have many more? Is the challenge with us? Is the challenge with our African potential partners? Why not more BITs?

Mr. LEO. I think there are two or three interrelated factors on this. One, it has not been a message that has emanated strongly from Washington that this is what we want to see happen. Instead, we have been talking about these trade and investment framework agreements which gather once or twice a year and we have a broad-ranging conversation but nothing that is particularly impactful. So I think it is a lack of political messaging that is coming from USTR and from Washington.

If President Obama had stood on the stage at the Business summit last August and said I invite every African government who wants to attract investment to negotiate a BIT with me, he would have gotten a lot of takers. So that is one challenge.

The second challenge is our new model BIT, our new template is very complex. It is complex for reasons. It is giving more public policy flexibility, but it is more difficult to negotiate now, particularly when you look at the other template agreements from our competitors. So that is a challenge we are going to have to address, but there are a couple of ways of doing that.

Senator COONS. Mr. Chairman, Mr. Bollyky wanted to respond, if he might.

Senator FLAKE. Yes.

Senator COONS. Please.

Mr. BOLLYKY. I just wanted to respond to the point on trade and investment. I am very supportive of increased trade and investment with sub-Saharan Africa. I spent much of my career working in USTR and negotiating such agreements. I am supportive for that reason.

That said, one other reason why you are seeing fewer investment agreements being concluded in sub-Saharan Africa is because of concerns over dispute resolution, which extend beyond sub-Saharan Africa, but they are particularly true in sub-Saharan Africa.

South Africa has begun a reevaluation process of all its BITs. It has withdrawn from several. That is going on. That reevaluation process of BITs has begun in other sub-Saharan African countries as well.

There has never been a dispute under an investor state that has found nondiscriminatory regulations to be expropriation. That said, there have been a lot of cases brought recently, particularly by the tobacco industry, and that has spooked countries, and that is what is really leading to this reevaluation process of investments treaties. There are a lot of concerns in these countries.

This concern is something that will be relevant for our ongoing U.S. trade negotiations and something to watch.

Senator COONS. And if I hear you right, in terms of the impact of health, reducing the rate of growth of tobacco use and consumption is probably one of the single biggest factors in noncommunicable disease growth in sub-Saharan Africa.

Mr. BOLLYKY. That is absolutely right. It is the second-leading health risk globally. Consumption is still relatively low in sub-Saharan Africa but is growing fast, and as incomes rise it is a big concern.

Senator COONS. Thank you very much.

Thank you, Mr. Chairman.

Senator FLAKE. Thank you.

Ranking Member Markey, you had a unanimous consent request?

Senator MARKEY. I thank you, Mr. Chairman. I would just ask to include in the record a report by the International Renewable Energy Agency entitled, "Africa's Renewable Future." The costs of wind and solar are falling dramatically. Globally, half of all new electricity capacity being added each year is renewable. So I think that we should just be prepared to be very, very surprised by how rapidly it grows, and I would just ask unanimous consent that it be included.

Senator FLAKE. Without objection.

[EDITOR'S NOTE.—The report submitted by Senator Markey for the record was too voluminous to include in the printed hearing. It will be retained in the permanent record of the committee.]

Senator FLAKE. I just want to thank the panel for your time. This has been extremely enlightening. Thank you for the valuable testimony, the innovative ideas. We look forward to following up with you. I just appreciate the time and effort you put into your statements, and also into your testimony here and answering the questions.

For the information of members, the record will remain open until the close of business today.

And with thanks to the committee, this hearing is now adjourned. Thank you.

[Whereupon, at 10:56 a.m., the hearing was adjourned.]

○